SOUTH WRIT LARGE

EDITED BY
AMANDA BELLOWS
KATHERINE DOSS
ROBIN MIURA
SAMIA SERAGELDIN

With additional editorial input by
Katharine Henry

Center for the Study of the American South
The University of North Carolina at Chapel Hill

SOUTH

STORIES, ARTS, AND IDEAS

WRIT

FROM THE GLOBAL SOUTH

LARGE

ISBN 978-1-4696-6856-7 (cloth : alk. paper)
ISBN 978-1-4696-6859-8 (ebook)

Published by the Center for the Study of the American South

Distributed by UNC Press
www.uncpress.org

For Professor James L. Peacock,
with gratitude for his unfailing support

CONTENTS

SOUTH WRIT LARGE

Hog Series CCLV: Red Rooster/Cardinal by Tarleton Blackwell, courtesy of the artist

MICHAEL MALONE

Introduction

I N AMERICA, there will always be "the South," as long as there is a south-erner left alive to define it. We will write it in books, paint it, protest it; sit on porches and at family reunions and Waffle Houses and golf clubs, at churches, campuses, courthouses and statehouses and talk it forever. Our mythical Souths. For the South has always been a big flexible myth and nothing lasts longer than a myth. Myths allow people to believe a lot of absolutely mutually exclusive things about their culture and therefore about themselves.

The painting (*Hog Series CCLV: Red Rooster/Cardinal*), an oil on canvas by the brilliant South Carolinian artist Tarleton Blackwell, captures the oxymoronic multiplicity of the southern myth: it's a portrait of a rooster boastful as the braggadocio Looney Tunes rooster Foghorn Leghorn, who was himself based on the blowhard southern politician Senator Claghorn from *The Fred Allen Show*.

Blackwell's rooster poses cocksure as General Custer in an elegant red uniform jacket, crowded with vainglorious military medals. He's like a Velasquez cavalier, or a leather-gloved Jeb Stuart, and he's posed in front of banners of sky and stars and bars. But there's a cardinal perched on his shoulder like a pirate's parrot, and the cardinal's claws are stars on the rooster's left epaulet. The cardinal is, of course, the state bird of Virginia, North Carolina, and Kentucky. The rooster is, of course, a food product, like Kentucky fried chicken.

The mythic South is always writ as large and as complexly as Blackwell's painting. Its soundtrack springs from "My Old Kentucky Home" and "Wayfaring Stranger" and "Shoo Fly," from field hollers and banjo blues to ragtime, jazz, soul, rock, pop, funk, and hip-hop, from Scotch-Irish ballads and spirituals, all these contributory streams flowing into the great Mississippi of American music with its deep African American roots. Our roots are "space and race," as Styron said, and they support our best gifts to art. They give us Huckleberry Finn and W. C. Handy.

In one guise or another, the myth of "the South" will always be reborn, redeemed or unrepentant, conceived as a lost dream or a cause indefensible, a struggle to be free, to go to hell for a good cause like Huck Finn. Like the unending fight for a national Ireland ("Erin Go Bragh—May Ireland Live Forever," "An Ireland Divided Will Never Be Free"), the South dreams backwards and forwards. This anthology is an effort to analyze at least parts of our complicated southern dream.

For cultural analysts, there are plenty of new regional mythologies—the Rust Belt, the West Coast, and the East Coast, but the myth of "the South" is among the oldest, perhaps the longest lasting, and so one of the most complex. It goes far back before John Smith's telling Jamestown colonists that if they didn't work, they wouldn't eat; back before the Colony of Georgia overturned their founder Oglethorpe's ban on slavery. It is about more than a civil war, bound to an origin story of displaced Natives, enslaved Africans, and usurping colonists.

In popular story, the South weds its American mythology to our other major nostalgic myth: the Old West or the Wild West. This imagined West has been broadly used around the world to define the fundamental character of the United States as a fiction of cowboys and Indians, outlaws and lawmen, everyone fast on the trigger. The West has had a greater impact than the South on international fashion (Levi's have traveled the world), on our motor culture (vans and trucks resemble covered wagons and stage coaches; cars and jeeps are named Cherokees, Comanches, Bisons, Broncos, and Mustangs), on our gun culture, our "don't fence me in" isolationism. And through Hollywood movies, westerns have provided a whole genre of globally exported myths. But we should notice that the South is writ large in this western narrative, that the West is rooted in the South. The western landscape is filled with displaced, defeated Confederates (like John Wayne in *The Searchers* or *True Grit*), with rural gunmen who found jobs as cowboys, sheriffs, US cavalry, rustlers and outlaws. Virginian Jesse James is as southern (and mythic) as Atticus Finch.

So maybe westerners are southerners who can't stay home or who can't go home again. The home-hungry who just think they can't go home again. Or the outsider who can never leave home and whose heart is always a lonely hunter.

This anthology tackles the complexity and diversity of southerners not by simply stitching together a large patchwork quilt but by developing an argument about how the South is writ large. The argument is not only chronological but accretive, accumulating new subject matter and adding to the old arguments of the Mind of the South.

Certain essays set the southern landscape in traditional ways like journalist Hodding Carter's "A Loyal Son of the South," and my own "Writing the South." Others use different parameters, like "Half-Drawn Hispaniola" by historian and novelist Katy Simpson Smith, a fascinating speculation on a partial hand-drawn map by Christopher Columbus upon seeing the new world: "It occurred to me that Columbus is kind of a southern story, if we embrace our Caribbean neighbors in a shared past. And what do southerners do if not remember things problematically?"

The section titled "Antebellum Legacies" invites a new generation of Civil War scholars including Clay Risen and John Dunn to bring contemporary analytic techniques and subject matters to old cotton fields and battlefields whose every inch has long been dug by generations of academic hoes.

"Cultural Cartographies," "Homelands," "Southern Afterlives," and "Culinary Kinships" go beyond the binary of black and white to give voice to other cultures brought by immigrants to the South. María Teresa Unger Palmer's "Mi Terra: Homeland for North Carolina Latinos." Malinda Maynor Lowery's "Recognizing Lumbee History Through Land." John Jung's "To Live and Die in the South: The Chinese Story." Katerina Katsarka Whitley, a Greek immigrant, writes of bringing her cooking to a small southern town: "The Flavors that Bind Us." Or we're asked to share in the experience of Ramesh Rao, an East Asian Indian immigrant, in "Georgia via Guntur."

Yet another perspective is that of the poems and illustrations throughout this anthology. There is also art criticism: the interpretations of a writer like Jill McCorkle on the painting of Bo Bartlett.

Again, it's not that southerners can't go home. It's that they always have to. We go home through our memories, we return to our childhoods, we visit our cemeteries. We go home when we re-experience our food, our cooking, our kitchens, our shared meals. It's been said that by knowing what we eat, we know who we are. Bill Smith's hard crab soup takes us home. Jaki Shelton Green's grandmother's hands in a mixing bowl take us home.

That's why collections like this one are invaluable. They are maps to who we were. And as Faulkner knew, the past is not even past. It's not just true for southerners.

Najee Dorsey, *Henrietta Lacks*, courtesy of the artist

CULTURAL
CARTOGRAPHIES

KATY SIMPSON SMITH

Half-Drawn Hispaniola

IN FEBRUARY, I found myself in Nashville with a few hours to kill before my reading at Parnassus Books. It was terribly cold, and weird pellets of slush were pinging off my windshield; I asked the audience that night about the phenomenon, and they told me it was sleet. I felt a renewed gratitude for my New Orleans home. In the midst of this frigid, wet assault, seeking shelter, I made my way to the Frist Center for the Visual Arts, a museum encased in an art deco former post office that's marbled with glamour. The exhibition on display didn't matter—I just wanted to thaw my toes—but it ended up being quite beautiful, pulling together a private Spanish collection that included works by Goya, Rubens, and Titian. This noble family also owned a folder of Columbiana, documents from those initial expeditions to the Americas in the 1490s: a ship manifest, a decree from Ferdinand and Isabella, and a travel diary from the winter of 1492–93 with a sketch of the northern coastline of Hispaniola.

I hovered over this map for a few moments then continued around the gallery, gawking at Goya's Duchess of Alba in White with its hilariously stoic lapdog. But a few minutes later I was standing again at the glass case, peering in. Just a simple sketch. Probably, though not certainly, by Columbus. Probably, though not certainly, the first map of the Americas drawn by a European. I was impressed, against my better judgment. (Where was the first map of Europe drawn by an indigenous American?) The image was captivating because it represented one of those flash points in history after which everything was irrevocably changed. That line in ink, drawn by a single man on a single ship sailing slowly past a coast, was also a line through the heart of the continent. Not a sketch but a garrote.

The map is small, but it takes up two pages of Columbus's travel diary, as if he misjudged the proportions when he began and ran over the crease in the binding with some chagrin. I can't help thinking he could have turned the diary ninety degrees and used his white space more efficiently. He may have thought the same. But this was more a placeholder than a piece of art. The line starts around the present-day town of Gaspar Hernández in the Dominican Republic, then snakes around the bumps in coastline (more prominent here than in actuality) until it rounds the western corner of Haiti and fizzles out near the present-day town of Gonaïves. Columbus is taken with the islands: Île de la Tortue is here ("Tortuga"), but also a cluster of three small islands near Cap-Haitien and a veritable archipelago near the peak of "Monte Cristi": a larger bean-shaped island and four whimsical satellites, each drawn counterclockwise. He deems the western cape "San Nicolas" and marks a single mainland town: "Natividad," or Villa de la Navidad, the fort his men built after the Santa María floundered on the reef. He was stuck there three weeks before finally escaping on the Niña. (When he returned a year later, the thirty-nine men he'd left had vanished, the settlement burned to the ground. Archaeologists are still poking around the Haitian coast searching for the ruins, the Hispanic Roanoke.) In and among the lines representing actual features are eight brown inkblots that exist in a cartographic twilight zone between island and bloodstain. They're precise enough for the former, and brown and clotty enough to shiver anyone who knows what Columbus brought to the Caribbean. From one of the stains a small cross grows: a sign of faith? A compass rose?

I didn't know what else was in the diary, and I wasn't particularly interested; Columbus's actual notes didn't hold any fascination for me. It's the map that was magnetic. It marked a story that had just begun; the continent's fate was being outlined—messily, hesitatingly. The fact that the map was unfinished drew the viewer in like a morbid counterfactual. Could things have gone differently? He's only half there. He's only so far in. No one knows what comes next.

This map only pops up in a few places when you search online. One is Yale University, on a webpage nestled in their Genocide Studies Program. Another is Southern Methodist University, where it advertises an exhibition on campus "celebrating Columbus Day weekend." It occurred to me that Columbus is kind of a southern story, if we embrace our Caribbean neighbors in a shared past. And what do southerners do if not remember things problematically?

What do we think we're celebrating on Columbus Day? That half-drawn line? The unknown that lures any explorer? The darkness that needs our own enlightened gaze? It's the impulse behind Manifest Destiny, colonialism, the Apollo missions: white people be conquerin'! Columbus's partial map is a drawing that invites our participation not only in the thrill of discovery but in the horror of what was to come. On the island of Hispaniola alone, 80 to 90 percent of the Taíno population died within a generation after Columbus's ships arrived. Some estimates put that at three million souls. As the great navigator bent over the desk in his cabin, tracing out the contours of a foreign land, his men were twisting through the forests, carrying guns and swords and viruses and Christianity and racism. For the Taíno, this was a story of genocide, not celebration. Yale got it right.

But the South, for all its memory problems, has a wealth of stories to draw from; Europeans weren't the only ones telling us what the world is shaped like. What about early American Indian maps? What do they look like? Circles upon circles upon circles, each linked by umbilical cords. Where Columbus drew a line and abandoned it, as far as his own knowledge reached, early maps from Catawbas and Chickasaws on the North American continent show the intricate relations between communities. There was no individual; there was no unknown territory. On a Catawba deerskin map from 1721, beyond the circles of towns, the English settlements to the north and south sit on the periphery, represented as squares. "This is our country," the map implicitly says, "and you are over there." (In addition to these sociopolitical maps, Native peoples created pictorial facsimiles of their physical environments as accurately as any European; Columbus himself encountered a Mayan man in 1502 who could chart sections of the coastline of Honduras.)[1]

West from Hispaniola, at about the same time Columbus was poking around the islands, the Aztecs were engaged in an interdisciplinary mapmaking venture of their own. The Codex Xolotl shows not just the mountains and rivers of the region but also its history: the arrival of the Chichimecs to Mexico, their exploratory jaunts through the terrain, and all the intricate dramas of a people in migration. There are speech bubbles, flipbooks of action, secondary plots. These maps are very much alive; the Aztecs had no interest in creating a static record of an unchanging natural world.

Maps reveal what a person, and the culture looming behind that person, thinks is important. Columbus wanted a precise rendering of Hispaniola's coastline, as far as his pen could reach. Why? So he knew where to land, how to retrace settlements, what he could claim. The Catawbas wanted a holistic picture of the peoples of the South; they needed to know where their friends and enemies stood, along what lines resources could be shared or traded, what a Catawba identity meant in a region of many identities. The Aztecs recounted a conquering history in order to legitimize their enduring presence in Mexico, link the people with the land, and shape communal memory. The indigenous mapmaking of the Americas tended to prize stories over data, a sense of fullness and completeness rather than the line that trails off because the individual's knowledge comes to an end.

And I, standing over a glass case in an old post office to escape the sleet of downtown Nashville—what did I need directions for?

I don't travel as much as I'd like. As a writer, I tend to be fairly stationary. Maps to me are games for the imagination: alternate worlds, a different set of eyes, might-have-beens. I imagine myself a tiny ink person traveling along this wiggly ink coastline— at a certain point, I fall off, like people told Columbus he would. His line takes me to the Caribbean. A map that depicts a location. His messy inkblots carry me to the cabin of his ship. A map of a man's body, the upset of his stomach, his shaky hands, a whispered "mierda!" His looped labels—Natividad, Monte Cristi—funnel me inside his brain: a map of the conqueror's hubris, a last flashing attempt at civilization before the ignorance and cruelty of his own people eradicate an entire culture, all those alternate maps destroyed before they could even be drawn.

I left the glass case and retreated to the far side of the gallery, where I pretended to look at a portrait of a woman in flounces while I watched the other patrons glide past the Columbiana display. Most glanced in the case for a second, scanning. Some, uninterested in pieces of paper, walked on by. One man stared for quite a while, then gestured excitedly to his wife, "Honey! Come check this out!" Could I blame him? I, too, hadn't been able to look away.

NOTE

1. Gregory A. Waselkov, "Indian Maps of the Colonial Southeast," in Powhatan's Mantle: Indians in the Colonial Southeast, rev. ed., ed. Gregory A. Waselkov, Peter H. Wood, M. Thomas Hatley (Lincoln: University of Nebraska, 2006), 435–502. See also Mary Elizabeth Fitts, "Mapping Catawba Coalescence," North Carolina Archaeology 55 (2006): 1–59.

MALINDA MAYNOR LOWERY

Recognizing Lumbee History through Land

LUMBEE HISTORY begins with the stories we tell about family and land. Those stories cannot be told apart from one another, for each gives the other meaning. Even as these elements reinforce each other, our history is also infused with contradictions, opposing forces that we must hold together in a tender kind of tension. Lumbees have built our nation to withstand these contradictions; we have learned that trying to erase them only reinforces the power of some at the expense of others.

Actually, *land* is hardly the right term for the Lumbees' home place—it is water and soil, two perfect opposites flowing together since ancient times. There are dense swamps where the water runs southwest, fingerlike, toward the river. But the river is not the wide Shenandoah or roaring Colorado; the Lumber River meanders slowly, twisting and turning an intricate design that changes periodically as her waters forge new paths.

In the Indian section of the county, seen from above, the Lumber River looks like a great snake, twisting and turning, swelling and breathing with the spring and summer rains. Snakes, in fact, have found a comfortable home there. Between the swamps there are wide, shallow basins that never dry out, called pocosins. European newcomers retained the word from our Algonquian ancestors; it translates to "swamp-on-a-hill." Pocosins are home to the Venus flytrap, the carnivorous threat to unwitting insects and a precious specimen to mystified humans. An equally charming, sweet-smelling vine, the Carolina jessamine, also makes its home there, entwining human hearts in its scent. But don't suck its nectar or eat its flower; you'll lose control of your muscles, your speech, convulse, and stop breathing—essentially the same symptoms of a poisonous love. Yet in the hands of particularly skilled healers, the vine's underground stem can cure the pains of love, especially migraines, fever, and menstrual problems.

Pocosin soil is peat, the vegetative material that becomes coal under proper conditions. Peat began forming 360 million years ago.[1] Like Lumbee women who will cry as they laugh, peat itself can burn when it's wet—burning peat is probably why one of our swamps is called Burnt Swamp. Our ancestors gazed at that peat fire, which burned indefinitely, beneath flowing water. Water would never put out that fire, so long as the peat was there to fuel it.

What spirits inhabit land where fire and water coexist, neither extinguishing the other? No wonder they dubbed one of these places a burning swamp; the name is a contradiction, and contradictions are reminders of how our history affects us. The land and its spirits have history too. We used to place our cemeteries at the edge of pocosins, perhaps because of the spiritual power we recognized there. We also planted a cedar tree, as cedar is the herb that heals—death, and its partner, eternal life, ultimately heal the body's frailties.

Centuries ago, our pine trees became partners with the swamps. Although the longleaf pine is mostly gone from our landscape today, we can remember a time in which it dominated. In 1524, Italian explorer Giovanni da Verrazzano described "immense forests of trees, more or less dense, too various in colors . . . too delightful and charming in appearance to be described."[2] The sandy well-drained soil in which longleaf pine grows best accompanied our rich peat: perfect opposites. The longleaf is an evergreen, like the cedar, and from a distance its needles look furry, soft, touchable. They are long and naturally curled, like a child's eyelashes; many Lumbee men retain those long, curly eyelashes into adulthood, making women mad for them and madly jealous at the same time.

All was forest and swamp, except for footpaths used to navigate through the dry places. The Lowry Road, also called the Mulatto Road, was one of the first of these paths to appear on English maps.[3] Local Indians and Natives from other places carved the Lowry Road. It runs from the Cape Fear River in Cumberland County into South Carolina. In the 1600s, Seneca hunters from Upstate New York may have traveled the Lowry Road as part of their search for beaver and their warfare against Catawbas and other communities in Piedmont Virginia, North Carolina, and South Carolina.[4] While the road became a place for migrants to travel, it was also a place for us to protect as a boundary that connected our family settlements and kept them hidden from view.

Like so many parts of Lumbee life, the road's contradictions made our power invisible and at the same time secured it. Just as our Lumbee and American history is a group of stories that we tell, it's also a collection of silences that we hide behind. The name Mulatto Road is but one example of such concealment. "Mulatto" is how outsiders described us, and it's a label that speaks to racial ancestry (Indian, Black, and white). But that label is not necessarily how we described ourselves because it does not represent kinship. "Lowry" represents people and relationships, not race, and so that is the name we have upheld, just as we uphold family.

Knowledge of family networks is another way we know who we are, encapsulated in the simple question a Lumbee will often ask when meeting another Lumbee, both at home and when the two have traveled to a far-off place: "Who's your people?" Southerners of all backgrounds use that phrase to narrow the distance between two people, but in the non-Lumbee world, it is often a test of social class, as if to say, "Is your family the same status as mine?" In other words, how powerful is your family compared to mine? Economics and politics are invested in that question. For Lumbees, the phrase tests a different kind of knowledge—an understanding of history. Often, we might find common ancestors three or four generations past, and then we usually ask another question: "Where do you stay at?" Often the answer is a community like Deep Branch or Union Chapel, one of the communities that has been central to our nation's structure since before the formation of the United States. This information yields another layer of knowledge, which informs relationships among people but also between people and places. Lumbees are a people because of our attachments to places, and our power is in our history.

The main roads, like the Lowry Road, took our ancestors in and out of our present-day homeland of southeastern North Carolina, and some of them were not from this particular place. Instead, many of our ancestors came from places all the way north to the James River in Virginia and south to the Santee River in South Carolina, east to the Atlantic Ocean and west to the Great Pee Dee and Catawba Rivers, an area of about seven thousand square miles. That territory is not ours today, but we are products of it nonetheless.

Our ancestors were not members of one nation, but from dozens that lived in this territory. The names of these diverse communities varied depending on where they lived and what Europeans wrote down about them. For example, the present-day Waccamaw Siouan people in North Carolina's Columbus County may have been called Woccon on British maps before relocating to their present homeland. Some of our Cheraw—also called Saura and Xuala—ancestors lived in and traveled through the present-day Lumbee homeland prior to the eighteenth century. Other Indians who moved to our present-day homeland were most likely refugees from as many as twenty different Indian communities, each with different names. All of these people spoke different languages and practiced different traditions from what scholars later called Algonquian, Iroquoian, and Siouan culture groups.[5]

The ethnic diversity of this area is hard to comprehend when US history teaches you that Indians are a "race" of people. We understand race today to mean that members of the racial group share a common culture and that the only differences might be in customs and attitudes, as in northerners are different from southerners. But before the settlers came, Indians in North and South Carolina and Virginia were enormously different from each other.

During the first two centuries of European exploration and settlement, those differences probably diminished according to the enormous destruction wrought quickly by disease. Lumbee ancestors probably began to die of diseases contracted from their Native trading partners before any of them ever saw any Europeans. The oldest members of the community, who kept our histories, died first, and the youngest members, who represent our futures, died second. The rapid and unexpected deaths of our elders and our children meant near instantaneous loss of cultural knowledge that had been accumulated for thousands of years, followed by the more gradual collapse of governments, languages, and every other commonality that keeps a nation together. Imagine what happens when an infectious disease kills 95 percent of your town, and you see why the intent may not have been genocidal, but the result certainly was. Yet there were survivors, and we are them.

NOTES

1. Thomas E. Ross, *One Land, Three Peoples: An Atlas of Robeson County, North Carolina* (privately printed, 1992), 34.

2. Giovanni da Verrazzano to King of France, published in 1841 by the New York Historical Society, with a translation by Dr. J. G. Cogswell, at "Giovanni da Verrazzano (Verrazzani)," Son of the South, http://www.sonofthesouth.net/revolutionary-war/explorers/giovanni -verrazzano.htm.

3. See, for example, *Map of Robeson County, North Carolina*, 1797, John Gray Blount Papers, North Carolina State Archives, North Carolina Maps http://dc.lib.unc.edu/cdm4/item _viewer.php?CISOROOT=/ncmaps&CISOPTR=3026&CISOBOX=1&REC=4.

4. For Seneca travels in North Carolina, see David La Vere, *The Tuscarora War: Indians, Settlers, and the Fight for the Carolina Colonies* (Chapel Hill: University of North Carolina Press, 2013).

5. The most comprehensive resource on this period of history is John R. Swanton, *The Indians of the Southeastern United States*, vol. 1 (Washington, DC: Smithsonian Institution Press, 1979).

RAMESH RAO

The Indian Experience in the South

Georgia via Guntur

ANY MAY NOT remember that Denzel Washington was a rising star when he was cast in the role of Demetrius, a self-employed carpet cleaner, in the 1991 small-budget movie *Mississippi Masala*. This movie, in which an African American man from Mississippi falls in love with an Indian woman and family tensions ensue, was one of the first tastes of the masala in the Indian American curry that the South experienced. Almost twenty-five years later, there were two Indian Americans, or "Asian Indians" (as we are officially labeled by the US Census Bureau), occupying governor's mansions in southern states. The two governors, Bobby Jindal and Nikki Haley, have even been considered potential presidential material, and so, surely, there must be some ingredient in the South that lends potency to the Indian presence in what has usually been considered hostile territory to many non-southerners.

Stories of the Indian immigrant to the United States are as varied and complicated as the myriad strands of Hinduism, and most are packaged in some stereotype or the other, benign or simplistic, malign or mistaken. Adding to the confusion are contemporary academics who prefer to label Indians "South Asians" because India was divided by the British into India and Pakistan in 1947, and therefore the new India is not the old India, and the old India now includes Pakistan and Bangladesh. So, their reasoning is why not lump all Indians together in an abstract and synthetic "South Asia?" This, however, causes confusion to nonacademics, who don't understand the differences between the "old" and "new" Indias. Any attempt therefore to present the essence of India is bound to be partial and unsatisfactory. We can only offer slices of that complex whole and hope that the reader will be tempted to make their own travel arrangements and discover for themselves the serenity undergirding the tumultuous ideas and realities of India. It is in that spirit that I have chosen to profile the six people in this essay—not as representatives of India or the New South but as windows that allow a peek into the old-new world.

India is an ancient land, and its modern inhabitants are citizens of the second most populous country in the world. Their home is the birthplace of Hinduism, Buddhism, Jainism, and Sikhism, and South Asia has the largest Muslim population in the world and is home to the majority of Hindus in the world. With about 2.5 percent of its population Christian, India has more Christians than there are people in Australia. To escape this complex and confusing tale, some Indians, born Hindu, converted to Catholicism. This enabled them to tell a simpler story of themselves, embellished to appeal to their majority Christian constituency. Others, born Sikh, did the same, and some now attend Christian churches. So, the United States is welcoming, it seems, if one is willing to both tell a simpler tale and make some major adjustments. And, if we are willing to remove the hyphen from our identity tags, we can all become Americans, they say.

The first Indians who landed on the shores of the United States in the early seventeenth century might have been brought here as slaves, and within a generation of the English setting up camp in Jamestown, there were English- and French-speaking Indian slaves who had been Christianized and who considered themselves a different class of slaves. How many of them survived, married, had children, and made a life for themselves, we don't know, and few of the Indian American historians now doing research in US universities seem to care to trace those stories. Between 1907 and 1909, about 6,400 Punjabi Sikhs, mostly male, illiterate, and unskilled laborers and agricultural workers, landed on the West Coast before the authorities called a halt to their immigration and locals harassed and tried to run them off. Many of them were persistent, however, and some of their descendants are now the biggest landowners in California.

Indian Americans are now considered the newest of immigrants, with the vast majority of us born outside of the United States, mostly in India but also from Britain, Africa, and the Caribbean. A Pew report shows that about 87 percent of Indian American adults were foreign-born and that only 56.2 percent of adults were US citizens. I find many of these more recent immigrants working for Aflac or TSYS in Columbus, Georgia, where most of them are techies—software engineers, designers, testers— who arrived during and after the high-tech boom of the 1990s, and especially during the period leading up to the doomsday scare of Y2K. A large group of these techies were recruited to do the basic debugging of computers and computer systems to ensure that there would be none of the cyber disasters imagined at the turn of the century.

Given that Indians came to the United States not to escape religious persecution, war, or natural disasters but in search of a better education and a better life, and that most arrived here after the 1965 Immigration Act that allowed people from around the world to make their way to the United States, Indians are among the most highly educated immigrant or ethnic groups—one of the, what is termed, "model minorities."

Those who came to the United States in the 1990s and afterward have not gone through the challenges that Indian immigrants faced when they first began arriving in the 1960s: the struggle to understand American colloquialisms and the difficulty of being understood; the expensive, short, once-a-month international phone call home; the eager wait for letters and small packets from home; the pangs of loneliness walking across a bare campus during spring or Christmas breaks; the hankering for home-made food; the challenge of understanding American ways and attitudes; the hand-to-mouth existence of graduate students and the joys of graduating and finding a job that liberated one from the servitude of graduate assistantships. While a graduate student in mass communication at the University of Southern Mississippi in the mid-1980s, I survived on a $4,500 stipend—half of which went to pay for tuition.

Recently, an Indian American professor of engineering who teaches at Auburn University was comparing his life with those of the new engineers and techies who are now arriving from India. These Indians are hired for short-term assignments and then stay on to find more lucrative offers by expert-starved US corporations. Our struggles, my friend reminisced, included graduate school's grueling rites of passage followed by the twenty- or thirty-year slow progress toward middle-class stability through hard-fought tenure, scholarly publications, difficult students, marriage in India, H1-B visas, green cards and citizenship paperwork, and the challenges of raising children in university towns. I remember some of us packing into a car to do the hour-and-a-half journey from Hattiesburg, Mississippi to New Orleans to buy Indian groceries, and then traveling six to eight hours to visit the Hindu temple in Houston. The expensive visits back home that happened once every two, three, or four years to attend a sister's wedding or to mourn the death of a parent were filled with bittersweet melancholia, and whatever little goodies we could take home to distribute among relatives and friends was always done with some trepidation and self-consciousness. These newcomers, we both enviously observed, endured or suffered little of that. Many of the techies have an undergraduate degree in engineering with technical experience already under their belts from India, and within a few years, if they decide to stay and work in the United States, their lifestyles would exceed our own. He and I both wondered about our different displacement experiences and mulled over our karma. Sure, each of the million or so Indian arrivals at American airports over the past six decades have their unique stories to tell, and few may have the inclination to write and talk about their immigrant experiences. But they are there for the curious to mine and explore, as Khyati Joshi has done in her scholarly work and as Bharati Mukherjee and Jhumpa Lahiri have done in their novels and short stories.

—————

Many of the newcomers, depending on their engagement with the larger society, know little of the history and culture of the South. That Martin Luther King Jr. invoked Mahatma Gandhi to help him shape the Black response to white racism, police brutality, and political chicanery barely registers with new Indian Americans. That he traveled to India in 1959 as a pilgrim in search of the holy grail of nonviolence and peaceful protest is but rarely discussed among us. In fact, very few Indian historians have explored King's remarkable visit to India.

Of the two million or so Indians living in the United States today, only about 50 percent are Hindu, despite comprising 80 percent of the Indian population. And while only about 2.5 percent of the Indian population is Christian, they constitute about 18 percent of the immigrant population. This might authenticate the claim by many that the United States is a Christian country. That the experience of Indian Christians in the United States is qualitatively different from the experience of other Indian Americans is noted by Khyati Joshi in her book *New Roots in America's Sacred Ground*, when she observes, "Christian research participants exhibit a qualitatively different set of experiences and responses in their relations with the dominant American culture" (46). In that context, it is equally important to note another observation she makes of Indian American religious groups: "Hindu research participants have a different construction of Indianness from that of the Sikh, Muslim, and Christian research participants" (46), which we can assume is because Hindus are a majority in India while Sikhs, Muslims, and Christians (minorities in India) find a release from the constraints of that minority status here in the United States, with those Christians identifying and acknowledging their newfound majority status here.

—————

The connection between India and the United States has other dimensions as well, for example, in the area of spirituality, meditation, yoga, and philosophy. In fact, Philip Goldberg, in *American Veda*, chronicles the history of the American interest in and engagement with the most profound and beautiful of India's contributions to the world in the forementioned fields. In the foreword to Goldberg's book, Huston Smith writes, "Early translations of Vedic texts found their way to America in the opening decades of the country's existence and influenced Jefferson, Adams, Emerson, and Thoreau . . . Vedanta quietly surfaces in the daily lives of Americans. Yoga, karma, meditation, enlightenment are now household words" (xiv–xv).

Before Swami Vivekananda, a young man, barely thirty, came to address the first World's Parliament of Religions in Chicago in 1893, some of the greatest American minds had already been seduced by the beauty and profundity of Hindu thought. After a circuitous two-month journey via China, Japan, and Canada, Vivekananda arrived in Chicago, six weeks before the inauguration of the conference, and stayed for four years, founding the Vedanta Society in New York City in 1894 as well as traveling to Britain in 1895 and 1896. He captivated some of the best minds in the West, including the famous physicist Nikola Tesla and the philosopher William James at Harvard, who offered the "Swami" a faculty position, which Vivekananda declined. Unfortunately, the farthest south that Vivekananda traveled within the United States was to Memphis, Tennessee, where he stayed from January 13 to 22 in 1894. Hailed as the "greatest figure in the Parliament of Religions" by the *New York Herald*, he was also treated with hostility in some towns, where "things were thrown at him."

Can we imagine what might have been Vivekananda's fate if he was invited to visit Jackson, Mississippi, or Atlanta, Georgia? Yoga and meditation groups can now be found in any town in any part of the United States, but there is also deep skepticism if not hostility to anything Hindu. Rev. Pat Robertson has even labeled Hindus "devil worshipers." But water shall carve and shape stones, and we now find an eighteen-foot-tall image of Lord Shiva installed by the Isha Foundation in a beautiful temple in the hills of southeastern Tennessee; the Swaminarayan Temple, a grand, shimmering marble palace of a temple built in Atlanta; and the Art of Living Foundation retreat and health center in Boone, North Carolina. Some eighty thousand Indian Americans make their home in the metro-Atlanta region, and they have a half dozen temples, large and small, that they gather in on weekends and on religious holidays, to bow and pray and conduct rituals, simple or profound, by trained priests or amateur householders.

It is difficult to stereotype Indian Americans though many have tried, including Hollywood. It seems strange that Hollywood writers cannot help but pigeonhole Indians as mostly petty shopkeepers, gas station and motel owners, or the occasional exotic "maharajas" who improbably feast on "eye-ball soup," as depicted in the movie *Indiana Jones and the Temple of Doom*. But times are changing and we now get a classic Hollywood sleight of hand with a character named Vincent Kapoor in *The Martian*. The name Venkat Kapoor, found in the book on which the movie is based, is itself improbable because Venkat is a South Indian name and Kapoor is mostly a Punjabi/North Indian surname, and when scouring any telephone book in any city in India you will not find one Venkat Kapoor. But America is chameleonlike, and there are new roles for the new Indian immigrants: the Aziz Ansaris, the Aasif Mandvis, the Kal Penns, the Kunal Nayyars, the Hari Kondabolus, and the Mindy Kalings who have begun to reshape American perceptions of Indians.

For example, Aziz Ansari, who grew up in South Carolina in a South Indian Muslim family, clearly breaks all stereotypes while confirming some as well: a doctor father, attendance at the state's top science and math school, and graduation from New York University's Stern School of Business. He has made it big both in stand-up comedy as well as on primetime television. That there are now more than a handful of stand-up comedians of Indian origin, and some who have made it very big, goes to show that not all Indians are gas station owners, or doctors, or Silicon Valley techies, or that our funny bones can't also tickle yours.

Every top business school in the country has a few Indian American professors, as does every top computer science, chemistry, physics, engineering, or medical department. Indian Americans are not just deans of the Harvard Business School or the Kellogg School of Management but can be found teaching in every kind of public and private university, small or large. There are not many Indian college and university presidents, but one of the first among them, Beheruz Sethna, headed the University of West Georgia for fifteen years.

And yes, there are doctors galore serving in big university-affiliated medical colleges, including at Emory University, and managing small-town clinics in Mississippi, Alabama, Georgia, and Louisiana. In fact, in Columbus, Georgia, there are nearly a hundred doctors of Indian origin in practice, and they are not just from the west-central state of Gujarat in India but are from all over, and represent every region and religion of the country—Hindu, Muslim, Christian, Sikh, and Jain—and speak in a variety of accents. Buttressing the stereotypes, however, are many, many gas station, motel, and convenience store owners, and many of them make the local news as they get held up or shot at, making fraught their relationship with the communities that sustain their businesses. Once in a while, a YouTube video goes viral as a brave but foolhardy Indian convenience store owner gives a gun-wielding youth more than he bargained for. In an interview, Bhumika Patel told local reporters that her Hindu faith gave her courage to fight back, which then undermines stereotypes about Hindus and their nonconfrontational ways.

Indeed, Hinduism is not an easy religion to understand, and it is not a religion in the mold of the Abrahamic faiths or any of the other prophetic, monotheistic religions that make monopolistic claims to the "one, true God." In this "rolling caravan of conceptual spaces, all of them facing all, and all of them requiring all" as Bibhuti Yadav once evocatively described Hinduism, one can imagine the Hindu tradition as a huge Banyan tree whose original roots are lost in time and whose new shoots were just born yesterday.[1] Gurus and godmen have made their way to the United States and have found much purchase, and while some may have sold spiritual snake oil, most of them have brought ancient wisdom and practices while finding new adherents who have thereby realized new meaning in their lives. And so it is that in a university town in the New South, a Christian priest marries a Hindu monk, confirming that despite strong-held beliefs, change has arrived in the South and yet another immigrant group whose rich and varied culture, history, and civilizational wisdom now leavens life in small-town Mississippi and in the governor's mansion in Columbia, South Carolina.

———————————

Immigrant groups go through change, and they settle down and their children grow up, become adults, date, and marry. What aspects of their parents' and grandparents' identities they retain and how much they assimilate become fodder for research and the occasional human-interest story in newspapers.

While we do not yet have the depth of research on Indian Americans that we have on Japanese Americans, for instance, we do know from some preliminary research that second-generation Indian Americans have different levels of commitment to their Indian American communities (see Khyati Joshi). For example, the Hindu American Foundation is a second-generation-led organization that seeks to represent the interests of Hindu communities in the United States. However, the level of interest and participation in its activities and efforts by second-generation Hindu Americans is yet to be carefully investigated and monitored. Given their light brown to deep-dark skins, Indian Americans may not be able to fully escape the usual queries, "So, where are you from?" or "What are your beliefs and who are your gods?" Indian Christians, Muslims, and Sikhs can respond to queries about their religious faith in different ways, depending on how strong their religious identities are and how closely they still identify with India. All of them, however, will have to struggle with parental concerns about who or whether they can date, and when and who and whether they can marry. It is commonplace now to find that Indian Americans date and marry outside of their religious and ethnic community groups: America's former surgeon general, Dr. Vivek Murthy is married to a Chinese American; Sri Srinivasan, who was among the short-listed candidates to replace Justice Antonin Scalia, is married to Carla Garrett, a Stanford classmate; Dr. Atul Gawande, the well-known surgeon, MacArthur Fellow, and best-selling writer of health and medicine is married to Kathleen Hobson; and Vanita Gupta, the top civil rights prosecutor and associate attorney general for civil rights is married to Chinh Le, a Chinese American.

———————————

The great poet W. B. Yeats once posed the philosophical and existential paradox: "How can we know the dancer from the dance?" The query is no different in the New South where many Indian Americans seek to discover and establish some Indian identity bragging rights. In this quest, there has been a rush to set up Bollywood dance studios where little girls and their mothers join the hip-swinging, chest-jiggling, rambunctious mishmash of gyrating dance set to loud music. Alas, when it comes to imports and exports, we can't predict what will sell, and thus Bollywood dance moves have become all the rage in clubs across Europe and now in the United States. Bad money pushes out good money, economists note, and in these times of the popular and the lowbrow, the wonderful dance and music arts of India have become marginalized as the onslaught by the Bollywood blight overwhelms all. Still, there are many connoisseurs who know, who enjoy, and who support the good and the beautiful, and while it is sometimes difficult to raise money to host a classical musician or a traditional dancer, some of us find ways to do so. Young men and women, trained in the best of the Indian arts, now study and perform this music and dance in colleges and universities across the country, and thus a fine sitar artist or a good vocalist can be found practicing late into the night in a college dorm room or in a little dance studio in a southern town.

Many of us have faced subtle or overt racism in our work lives, and some of us have attracted the jealous, if not envious, attention of colleagues or neighbors—and that is par for the course for almost all immigrant groups in the United States. A few therefore have returned home because India now provides many more opportunities to grow and prosper. But as we grow older and our identity struggles take on a sharper edge, we lie awake at nights wondering why we made the journey, what we gained, and how much we have lost. The best accounting experts will not be able to keep a good or fair tally, and so we must wait for the inspired raconteur to tell us about her immigrant life, of the freedoms she enjoyed, and the familiarity of the ancestral home she lost. Some of us straddle cultures with aplomb, and many of us have tucked our memories away quietly into a forgotten photo album. As Salman Rushdie said, it is not in the nature of human beings to "perceive things whole" and we are "capable only of fractured perceptions."

So be it, or as we say in Sanskrit, "Tathaastu."

WORKS CITED

Goldberg, Philip. 2010. *American Veda: From Emerson and the Beatles to Yoga and Meditation— How Indian Spirituality Changed the West*. Harmony Books.

Joshi, Khyati. 2006. *New Roots in America's Sacred Ground: Religion, Race, and Ethnicity in Indian America*. Rutgers University Press.

Rushdie, Salman. 1991. *Imaginary Homelands: Essays and Criticism 1981–1991*. Viking Books.

Takaki, Ronald. 1989. *Strangers from a Different Shore: A History of Asian Americans*. Little, Brown.

Yadav, Bibhuti S. 1980. "Vaisnavism on Hans Kung: A Hindu Theology of Religious Pluralism," *Journal of Religion and Society* 27: 60.

PAULETTE BOUDREAUX

A Steady Stream of Leavers

HEN I WAS a child in Laurel, Mississippi, in the 1960s, in the years before I set foot in America's Great Migration stream and let it wash the native soil from my roots and carry me to California on a tide that had already carried millions of Black Americans away from the South, I remember watching the Black teenaged boys, with their swagger and ambition, grow restless with boredom and the racist Jim Crow system that circumscribed their lives. The ones who made good on the boast of their swagger enlisted in a branch of the US military or boarded a Greyhound bus heading straight north like Canada geese to places like Chicago and Detroit. Sometimes they came back to visit, looking spit-shined and polished, with tales of glamour and prosperity about life lived elsewhere. Sometimes they came back more defeated than when they left, with bad habits and the burdensome shame of having failed to make it up North. Mostly they didn't come back. They were just gone, swallowed up in that magical Promised Land that the world outside of the South represented for me then.

My mother tells me that it wasn't just the teenaged boys that migrated north. It was teenaged girls and whole families too. She remembers a steady stream of leavers from the time she was a girl growing up on a sharecropping plantation with her parents and six siblings in the 1930s and '40s in rural Mississippi. She says she never thought she would become one of the leavers.

But she did. The whole family did. We uprooted ourselves and became migrants—part of the permanently displaced in search of the American Dream.

In *The Warmth of Other Suns*, Isabel Wilkerson notes that some six million Black Americans left the South for points north, east, and west between 1914 and 1970. They were all looking for better lives for themselves and future generations. Some succeeded and some failed. For the migrant there is never any guarantee that one will thrive in the new land. But that prospect of failing doesn't stop the yearning that calls people to voluntarily migrate, seeking greener pastures. My own story is an example.

Growing into adolescence in Mississippi, I developed a quiet ambition and swagger of my own, and I started to feel restless like other teenagers before me—though the word *migration* wasn't part of my vocabulary and I wasn't interested in the North so much as I was interested in the places I read about in the books I checked out from the library. I was interested in traveling to places like Paris and New York City and Boston. I wanted a life different than what seemed easily available for a female like me growing up among the working and abject poor in my small, racially segregated Mississippi town.

At first I had lived, without much thought, inside the lines that were drawn for me by the facts of my gender, my family's financial struggles, and the dangers of the racial divide, those "separate but equal" policies that defined the circles inside which I could live my life. But having been an avid reader from an early age, I understood that there was much more to the world than what was offered in my hometown. And as I got older and my awareness extended beyond my insular community, I found myself wanting some of that "more"—more material goods, more freedom, more options. But how would I get more? All indicators seemed to point toward leaving.

My mother was the second oldest of seven children in her family. When she was seventeen, her mother died. A year later, her father died. My mother and her older sister joined forces with their maternal grandmother to continue raising the five younger siblings—four boys and one girl. Over the next few years, my mother's brothers grew to be restless, ambitious teenaged boys who were not content to toil as field workers on someone else's farm or work in one of the local lumber mills—the primary work available to them as young Black men in that part of Mississippi. So one by one, as they got old enough, they joined different branches of the US military. My mother remembers signing papers for one brother who was not yet eighteen when he was ready to enter the military, so eager was he to get away from what would have been his fate had he stayed. My mother watched them go—two to the Army and one to the Air Force. They fanned out across the United States and circled the globe.

It took them a while to remember home.

My uncles returned in the late summer just before the start of my tenth-grade year. The oldest one had been gone for more than fifteen years. After his stint in the military, he had settled in San Francisco and taken up work as a longshoreman on the waterfront there. The second in line spent his time in the military working in telecommunications. Upon leaving the service, he parlayed the knowledge and skills he had acquired into a well-paying, well-respected career with the phone company in San

Francisco. The third one was about ten years into what would become a twenty-seven-year military career.

From my teenaged perspective, the three of them were all spit-polished and shined, dapper in the way they dressed, like the boys who came back to visit from up north to brag about the better lives they had up there. My uncles' English was smooth and refined with nary a trace of rural Mississippi in it. Their wallets were full of money that they spent freely on us for food and school clothes. They even arranged to pay the private transportation fee for me and my cousin, who was the same age and in the same grade as me, to ride the several miles we would have had to walk to get from our house to the only Black high school in my segregated town. My uncles reassured us that their money would be easily renewed when they returned to their respective permanent jobs and homes, worlds away from mine.

In the week and a half of their visit, they followed us around in our daily routines. By this time, my stepfather was no longer in the picture, and we were a single-parent family of eight children (six of us belonging to my mother plus two cousins, the children of her older sister who was killed in a car accident a few years earlier). My mother had work on a processing line at a poultry processing plant. The pay was much better than the domestic work she had done for most of my early childhood. Her single income now surpassed what she and my stepfather, a farm and construction laborer, used to bring home together. We had moved to a bigger house, and though we didn't think of it this way, we were still living on the edges of poverty—"going nowhere fast" as one of my cousins would later say. It was the shocked and distressed responses of my uncles to our lifestyle that really threw our circumstances into relief. Their conversations highlighted the grave economic inequities between life on the Black side of town and life on the white side, the harshness of the racial lines we had to tow, the growing tension around the outside push to desegregate the public schools, and the still limited job prospects for young Black people especially.

My uncles had been away too long, they said. They had forgotten just how difficult life was for Black people in our little corner of Mississippi—the poverty of so many, the discrimination against all. Their visit had reminded them why they left and what it was they had left behind. They were pained to think of part of their family struggling under the harshness of life in Mississippi in 1969. So when the two uncles who lived in California went home, they started hatching a plan to get us all out. They said it would take them a couple of years to pull together the money to fly the nine of us out (my mother, my siblings, and my cousins) and get us set up with a place to stay.

The plan changed when the school desegregation issue in Mississippi heated up in early 1970. The federal government was forcing the issue, and the state and policy-makers in my town began discussing overhauling the school system to accommodate the government mandate. There was talk of the schools shutting down and teachers going on strike, and there were threats of violence on both sides of the tracks. What concerned my mother and her brothers were my female cousin and I who were finishing up tenth grade that year. My mother had always leaned on the notion, and pushed it heavily, that education was the magic potion that would help to float us above the poverty and chaos and stunted possibilities for most Blacks in our town. If the schools were shut down in protest, or teachers refused to teach, we would not be able to finish high school in time. And what kinds of trouble might we, restless teenagers already, fall into with empty time on our hands and no prospects for moving forward in life? Neither my uncles nor my mother was comfortable with the thought of our succumbing to early motherhood and marriage or joining in the active fight for civil rights going on all around us in our hometown and other parts of the South. So behind the scenes my mother and her brothers decided that my cousin and I would go to California after finishing tenth grade and enter eleventh grade in San Francisco.

"You two are at that age where you need to start thinking about the future," my mother said when she introduced this plan to us. "I want something better for y'all than what I've had. Things are better for Black folks in California. More doors will be open for you there."

My cousin and I didn't even need to let the air cool around her words. My mother didn't have to convince us. We had already assessed what awaited us in Mississippi. Some of our high school friends were already dropping out of school to have babies, and most Black women who worked outside of their own homes, which was most of them, were working in some type of domestic or caretaker jobs, or in food industry or agriculture. Our uncles were offering us the possibility of entry into that wider world, the golden Promised Land of California. Even better than "up North," my cousin and I agreed. Of course we would go for this shot at a better life! We would move to California, even though it meant that we would have to live with our longshoreman uncle and his wife and three children for at least a year. It would take that long for him and our other uncle who worked for the phone company to save money to bring the rest of the family out.

In the summer of 1970, my cousin and I boarded a nineteen-seater airplane heading for California at the small airport in my hometown. In the fall of that year my town's decision about how to integrate the public schools brought with it massive upheaval in the school system and overt racist violence. From the safety of my uncle's home in San Francisco, my cousin and I heard reports of the ordeals my three school-aged younger brothers and her brother faced while being bused to schools on the white side of town.

A year later in the summer of 1971, my mother and the rest of my immediate family boarded the same nineteen-seater airplane my cousin and I had taken and headed west. We had come to California with the usual migrants' hopes for a better life and a real shot at the American Dream.

In theory the migrant in America has moved to a place that has the same language, the same laws, the same government as the place she left behind, but in reality, to move from one region of this great country to another is to traverse into foreign territory where the laws are not really the same. Each state government has its own laws and rules, and the federal laws get interpreted differently in different places. Look at how Mississippi had skirted the federal laws from the time of *Brown v. Board of Education* in 1954 until 1970. This kind of individualized interpretation of the world extends to the spoken language as well. Even English is interpreted differently from place to place.

So migrating within the United States calls for reconfiguring, reimagining, and finally reinventing one's self. This reconfiguring is no simple task, but the hopeful migrant is so anxious, so eager to fit, to belong, so sure that her ability to gain all that this Promised Land has to offer depends on her facility at adapting, that she will do it. As she adapts and reinvents and acquires the accoutrements of this new land, she must give up some things, some of which she doesn't even know the value of yet. She gets busy letting go and trimming and reshaping herself to fit the contours and tongue of the new land. This was especially so coming from the South in a time when the televised version of the civil rights movement was still running hot, keeping fire to the notion that Blacks from the South were all to be pitied, tolerated, and taught how to be full humans. It was also before presidents Jimmy Carter and Bill Clinton had shown Americans outside the South that not everyone from the South was a low-IQ country bumpkin.

When I arrived in San Francisco, it felt as though I were no longer in the same country, so vast were the differences between the deep South of the Mississippi I had left and the far West of the California where I now found myself.

The language was the same, sort of. I understood the people around me. They spoke the kind of English I was used to hearing on the television and in the movies. Their speech sounded like the English I read in books. But many claimed not to understand my southern English or my idioms. And when they did understand me, they dismissed my southern speech as quaintly funny and focused on the humor instead of what I was saying. The slow musical rhythm of my speech was taken not as cultural norm but as a sign of a slow intellect. In either case, I was not to be taken seriously. Though I was aware that I was neither quaint nor dull-witted, I was working against others' perceptions. I decided that I would have to learn a whole new English and new ways to use the English I had.

Through careful listening and imitation, I learned to change the pronunciation of most of my vowels and to put accents on different syllables than the ones I had learned in grade school. And I learned to hurry over some words, not even pronouncing all their syllables, never giving them time to luxuriate in my mouth before rolling off my tongue and into the world. I learned to be more direct and less pictorial in my speech. I learned to say, "you guys," instead of "y'all" even when referring to a group of girls. Speaking in these ways to avoid standing out so much from my classmates at my new high school meant suppressing my mother tongue. It sometimes meant a few seconds of lag time while I translated a thought from my southern Black English into a California regional neutral English. But with time I acquired the new English, or so I thought. I have come to realize that I am in fact a sort of bilingual with an internal monologue that has the cadence and idiomatic nature of southern speech. This inside language sometimes finds its way into the outside world in blatantly recognizable ways, and I have been told by people who pay attention to speech patterns that I have not been entirely successful in scrubbing out the rhythm and pronunciation of my mother tongue, that it is there undergirding my speech, and more apparent when I am in certain moods, or tired, or stressed.

This possibility of letting southern-sounding words or idiomatic expressions slip out and betray my Mississippi background was a source of high anxiety when I was first acclimating to my new world.

Language was but one of the pieces of my life that I needed to become conscious of and to modify if I wanted to survive comfortably in this new land where I had no roots, no specific community, no history of any kind to fall back on. There were customs and mores in this big western city that differed significantly from those of small-town Mississippi. From the simple courtesies of saying "Yes, ma'am" and "no ma'am" to elders and greeting each person I encountered, especially other Black people, with "Good morning" or "Good evening," to the more complex questions of how, as a young Black female, to interact with the solicitous white salesclerks in the major department stores downtown, or the Chinese family who ran the corner store and laundry service at the end of our block, or the white boy in my American history class who asked me out on a date.

Food and the culture around preparing and consuming it was a whole other area of life that was different in California than in Mississippi. A lot of the foods we were accustomed to in the South simply were not available. And then there was a whole world of foods that we had to acquire a palate for—foods like avocados, broccoli, and tacos. In the first few years we were in California, my mother had the hardest time searching grocery stores all around the city trying to find the ingredients for traditional holiday meals such as hog-jowls, ham hocks, black-eyed peas, and collard greens for the New Year's feast.

Clothing and the appropriateness of certain items of clothing for specific occasions were another issue. We would show up to events dressed in what would have been the right attire back home, only to be laughed at, teased, or ignored because our "country hick" was showing. My mother, a regular Baptist churchgoer before we left the South stopped going to church after a few tries and getting the sense from various encounters that she was being judged harshly because her Sunday best was out of place. Eventually she found a denomination that was accepting of her, but it took years.

The fast pace of life also took some adjustment. Coming from a cultural reality where life moved at an easy pace, where the journey often seemed more important than the destination, it was hard to appreciate the fact that everyone was so often in a hurry and stressed by the fact of time. In this new land, one was penalized and judged harshly for not living life like it was a fifty-yard dash, and some people took my easygoing attitude toward time as a personal affront.

But in some ways, what took the most adjustment was the way in which coming from a small Mississippi background of deprivation where so much was denied to me made me hungry for every bit of everything that was now opened and laid out before me like a smorgasbord. I took nothing for granted—from the material to ethereal—nothing. I was open to all sorts of experience, including uprooting myself again and stepping once more into a migrant stream when my high school counselor encouraged me to apply to and attend an East Coast university.

What came much later for me was an understanding that by working so hard to fit, to belong in the new place, I was erasing important parts of my identity. The problem with that kind of erasure is that there are so many different ways that a migrant, just like an immigrant from another country who arrives beyond a certain age, is never fully at home in the new land. (Some psychologists will tell you that the certain age is around six or seven. Some psychologists and social scientists will tell you that if you are raised by people who migrated or immigrated when you were just a gleam in your parents' eyes when they arrived at the new place, your interior self will still be constructed on the foundation of that native place, which dictates the inflections in your parents' words and the unguarded manners and behaviors in the home and the parents' philosophical orientation to the world.) This never feeling completely at home inevitably causes one to bump up against the question of identity—the question of "who am I really?" If one has done too good a job of erasing, the answers are difficult to excavate. Thus the migrant is often left with the sense of being permanently displaced, always a little bit on the outside, even when one has learned the customs and the language of the new land and it no longer feels foreign.

Perhaps I am assigning too much to all migrants from my own migrant experience. But what I know is that migrants tend to gravitate toward people with similar roots who offer even a whiff of the homeland. For example, my cousin and I survived our first year of high school life in California by forming our own little clique of girls who were as fresh off the boat as we were—two sisters also from Mississippi and one girl from Arkansas. My uncles all married women who were also migrants from the South. And through my times of zigzagging across the county, calling different places home, I have often encountered other displaced southerners who, regardless of race, class, and gender identification have sought to connect on the basis of our shared childhood culture, for the South is like no place else.

But the shared migrant experience also crosses regional lines. At times I have connected with people who moved from other parts of the country besides the South. Sometimes what was shared was simply the fact of not "being from here," wherever "here" happened to be. The connection was around knowing the experience of moving from one part of America to another, suddenly feeling like a stranger in a strange land and needing to reinvent and design a new self for the new location. Even when the migration is voluntary and desired, there is still a complicated reckoning that must happen.

My family did get a nicer slice of the American Dream Pie once we left the South— a few college degrees among us, home ownership, better jobs and good careers, more freedom to set our own paths through life, and in general more options and optimism for future generations. But we all still behave like displaced persons in one way or another, still relating to that mythic home, whether running away from it and its memory, or running toward it as two of my siblings have done by moving back to Mississippi.

When I visit the South and I find comfort in the rhythm of the language and the pace of life, I feel my roots relaxing and pushing in to familiar soil. But I am also aware that my experiences as a migrant adapting to different lands have made me into a hybrid of sorts—an American with branches from different parts of the country grafted on to the original plant, belonging at once to Mississippi and California—and belonging at once to neither.

Clementine Hunter, *Mural at the African House* c/o Cane River Art Corporation

ANTEBELLUM LEGACIES

W. HODDING CARTER III

A Loyal Son of the South

I GREW UP IN A HOME in which guns were as familiar as Franklin Roosevelt—and considered by my father as indispensable as FDR to our welfare and security. I grew up in the Mississippi-Yazoo Delta, hundreds of thousands of acres of unbroken floodplain stretching from Memphis to Vicksburg. It was protected from the Mississippi River's annual rising tide by a fragile levee system that had given way in 1927 to a flood that covered the land for five months.

It was "the South's South," as novelist Richard Ford phrased it, and its white minority held passionately to the creed of white supremacy. Affecting the planter's mantle, most of its white farmers had but recently wrestled the land from swamp and thick forest and yellow fever. Affluence for whites was rare; abject poverty for Blacks who toiled the land as serfs was endemic.

My father was as loyal a son of the South as the South ever produced, save for two qualities. He never stopped growing, and he would not march in lockstep in a white society that valued—no, demanded—conformity behind the segregationist creed.

Let me be very clear here. My father was no liberal, as that term is and was understood on the Upper West Side of Manhattan or in Harvard Yard. The title of a well-researched biography of his life was *The Reconstruction of a Racist*. It was a marketing ploy, that title, one that I resent to this day, but it embodied a home truth. The grandson of one of the founders of the post–Civil War Ku Klux Klan—or so family legend had it—he held to all the tenets of white supremacy throughout his high school and college years.

But he was afflicted with intelligence and nurtured in the democratic creed and the Christian faith, strictly Southern Presbyterian though it was. He could not square either one with the raw, brutal repression of the Black man. No integrationist, he nevertheless could not understand why the education and employment of Black Mississippians was a threat to white civilization—or why those who were qualified to vote should not be allowed to vote.

Which is what he wrote, practically from the moment he founded his second daily newspaper in Greenville, Mississippi, in 1936, squarely nestled against the levee that had been ripped apart just nine years earlier. It is what he practiced in what he chose to cover and how he covered it.

And it provoked rage and threats, advancing and retreating in response to what his tiny daily offered up to its readers from week to week. Thus the guns—an implicit bulwark against incessant midnight phone calls and direct encounters, frontier fashion, with men who loved to brawl and hated "n——— lovers"—that despicable label for the white nonconformist.

Dad went off to war, his National Guard unit called into service by Roosevelt thirteen months before Pearl Harbor. What he later experienced of the world's nonwhite majority during the North African campaign and the conclusions he drew from the war against fascism focused his general unease into clearer distinctions about what was acceptable and unacceptable here at home. In a white-hot six months as he was leaving the service in 1945, he wrote a series of editorials that won him the Pulitzer Prize and earned the undying, unremitting enmity of the racist majority.

Which is where I came in. Back from a sprawling apartment complex built in suburban Maryland to house the huge wartime influx, I was reintroduced to my white grammar school peers in the Delta as a boy with a Yankee accent, a weird name, and a communist, "Jew-bought" (Pulitzer was Jewish), "n——— lover" father.

It was an introduction I tried desperately to evade. Call me Will, I begged of my folks. Cool it with the editorials—please? Let me blend into the background. All to no avail. While most of my classmates eventually saw me in more complicated ways, there would always be the sneering bully boys who, learning at their parents' knees, tried their best to drive me out of the schoolyard and then out of all the community haunts so dear to teenagers.

It didn't work on Dad and, thanks to his example, it didn't work on me. Not in the 1940s and not in the 1950s and 1960s, after the Supreme Court's *Brown v. Board of Education* decision of 1954 and his editorial endorsement of its inevitability. Not ever during the sixteen-year segregationist boycott of the newspaper that only ended in 1969, when it had become inescapably clear that a lone newspaper editor in a smallish Delta town was not responsible for the black revolution and federal intervention.

Despite all those nights sitting outside with guns, waiting for the night riders to come, none ever did. A stray burning cross here, some smashed windows there, garbage on the lawn after my brother accidentally killed himself in 1964—these were the sum and substance of physical assault.

As for the attempt to destroy us economically, it failed. It did not succeed because Dad knew implicitly, and I learned by osmosis, that being out of step need not be fatal if you were simultaneously working and advocating for the common good. They couldn't destroy him, they couldn't destroy the paper, and they could not, later, destroy me because we always were of community, deeply involved in community, concerned about the community's future. As the old joke went, we might be SOBs, but we were *their* SOBs, and we wrapped that town around us like a blanket against the storm. And they could not destroy his or, later, my will because of the other great lesson he taught and I learned. Unless you were a psychopath or a fool, being afraid in the face of unremitting threats and pressure was inevitable. But being afraid was not the end of the story. It was the beginning.

Bravery does not arise from ignorance of the consequences or reckless disregard of them. It is the definition of action taken in the wake of fear and in full awareness of the possible consequences. Seeking fearless heroes is a feckless enterprise. Mastering fear and soldiering on: That is bravery.

What of faith in all this? At core, it was and is everything. Dad was a fallen Presbyterian, grandson of a stern Calvinist who had presided over her huge brood's table with rigorous rules and stern moral pronouncements. He was lured away to the spiritual lassitude (that's a joke from a practicing Episcopalian) of the Episcopal Church by his young New Orleans bride. But whatever the sign on the church door, what he derived from faith was encapsulated in the two great commandments. For Dad, that was Christianity's eternal guidance. The Fatherhood of God and the Brotherhood of Man.

But the organized church was and remained in cultural captivity for generations across the South. Preachers quoted scripture to defend segregation no less than they had defended slavery. Men stood at the church door not to welcome all to worship a common God but to repel those whose skin color was closer to that of the biblical Jesus than of theirs. The Social Gospel was reviled as Marxist by many. It was a shameful, sordid chapter in church history. For those Christians, the sad joke applied. "But Daddy, you know what Jesus would say about segregation," said the young woman home from college. "Yes," Daddy replied, "but He would be wrong."

The following will not be a long recital of war stories. I came back to our Delta newspaper from the Marines in 1959. I took over editorial control in 1962 and became editor in 1966. My father went through a long, tragic decline in the last ten years of his life, dying at age sixty-five in 1972. He never saw the total collapse of "our way of life," of the braying jackasses of racist demagoguery. But he saw enough to know that while he had been out of step with his region for so long, it had finally been brought more nearly into step with the demands of America's democratic creed and religious heritage. He may not have won, but his enemies—the enemies of human decency, of Christianity, of our democratic imperatives—had lost.

Thus, my first enduring lesson as my father's son and a southerner of a certain time: If you really care about a place, a region, a nation, you refuse to accept its dark side or succumb to its conformist blandishments. At the same time, you never fall into the error of believing that it is somehow uniquely sinful in an otherwise sin-free land. To believe that is to ignore history.

Which leads to my second lesson as my father's son. No political position or ideology is entitled to unblinking acceptance. Truth is not the monopoly of any one person or people or region or nation. All of mankind being fallen, none can demand tribute as unassailable.

I have pretty much been an unblinking Democrat all my life—insofar as how I usually vote. But no Democratic president or Congress has deserved or received a free pass from Hodding Carter the journalist, younger or older, and in the early days of building a two-party system in the South, a number of Republican candidates received our editorial endorsement. Support for a two-party system arose from familiar roots. If the abuse of power in the name of revealed truth is unacceptable, it is equally true that political power unchecked by vigorous competition and regular defeat will be abused. Absolute power corrupts absolutely. Always.

The magnificent political principles embodied in the founding documents and the moral imperatives embedded in the two great Testaments deserve our unblinking allegiance. But to march in lockstep behind any single person or faction, to confuse the nation with an individual or party, is to commit cardinal error. When we put on team jackets, we give up free will and individual conscience. Each of us has an inner drummer. Each of us must pay heed to its beat, even when it means marching counter to the great parades of the moment.

There were other derivative lessons I drew from my dad's example—no matter how belatedly or reluctantly. Passionate belief is no guarantee of truth. Good intentions can mask vile behavior. There is more than one way to reach a desired objective.

Over the course of my career as a journalist, I wrote some 5,500 editorials. I wrote perhaps five hundred columns, dozens of magazine articles of one kind or another, and a handful of books. When I wrote each of them, I thought I was right. When I wrote many of them, I was passionately certain that I was doing God's work. I was no less passionately sure that those who disagreed were in fundamental error. I even thought that some of them represented, as the President George W. Bush once described our international enemy, nothing less than evil incarnate.

I have tried to apologize for that mindset repeatedly over the past decade or so. In retrospect and almost inevitably, many of those editorials were written in haste and published in error. Much of my moral fervor was so much hot air. Some of the positions against which I railed I later came to embrace—whether about the war in Vietnam or the War on Poverty. And some of those I hailed as champions of the good and right were later revealed to be corrupt or weak or downright villainous. Error turned out to be a commodity that did not respect party labels. It would have been far better for my readers and my sense of self if I had heeded my inner voice more closely, if, in the grip of certainty, I had not stampeded with a temporary majority or saluted a false banner. Christian faith and democratic precept: Both are clear on this subject. No one has a monopoly on truth or virtue. *Gott mit uns* is blasphemy. The point of democratic politics is to curb the inevitable reign of error that comes with fallible human judgment and power too long in the saddle, no matter whom it professes to serve. It requires a different kind of bravery to acknowledge your own error and that of your ideological or political comrades in arms, and it is a bravery often no less difficult to muster than the physical kind. At end of the day, after all, it means you are out of step—and being out of step is always painful.

That great chronicler of southern politics and mores V. O. Key once wrote directly to the larger point: "Ruling groups have so inveterate a habit of being wrong that the health of a democratic order demands that they be challenged and constantly compelled to prove their case."[1] That is a precept that should hang in every newsroom, in every classroom, and in every home.

Talking about a seemingly distant past, about old preceptors and precepts, can be a way to avoid encountering the perplexing controversies of the present. Preachers in the pulpit and on the editorial page can thunder eloquently about sin but miss the sinful realities of contemporary public life and of national policy. Old stories can substitute for hard choices in the here and now. There are such choices aplenty for each of us to make today, but the glory of our current scene is that the fear that accompanied dissent in times gone by has itself gone with the wind. Editors in this country do not have to carry weapons as they go about their rounds, if anyone even bothers to notice what they are writing. I emptied the last pistol and put up the last rifle in my house in 1965.

There is no excuse today for any of us to turn away from speaking truth to power—or at least, we cannot legitimately claim to fear for our lives if we do so. That is a situation reserved for the incredibly brave men and women who continue to speak out in those dozens of countries where the state is God, where religious fascism calls down fatwahs against dissenters or corrupt, market-eager communist cadres silence freedom of speech wherever it shows above the Internet horizon. There is no excuse in this land except the human one—*I want to be accepted, to be loved, to be included,* to be embraced by the many.

Which takes me back to Dad. I said he loved the South, and he did so, passionately. He loved this country, losing an eye in its service. He loved approbation.

But he put all at risk, repeatedly, because he loved something else even more. He loved what his country held out as its central promise and premise. He loved what his region could be if it would but pay heed to the core elements of the religion it embraced with such religiosity. And he taught his sons to try to feel the same way, and to try to act accordingly.

The fact of the matter is that our history, our common Father, demands no less. Ours is a living faith or it is nothing. Ours must prove itself to be a democratic nation in the way it acts in the here and now, rather than through its monuments and little-noticed holidays, or it is a hollow husk.

To get it right almost invariably means breaking step with current fashion, current power, current certainties. It means marching to your own drummer. It means facing down the crowd.

And doing all that does not actually guarantee it will come right. Being sure you are right is not the same as being right. Bravery entails risking error in the pursuit of truth.

Nevertheless, the one guarantee that history offers and that I learned from Dad's example is that if we give up on the effort, it will never come right. Happily, we of the South in particular know that seemingly intractable situations can be redeemed. Saved by the grace and courage of the oppressed, we were given a chance to rise above our past, and we continue to do so. We owe it to ourselves and them to confront our present age with the same prophetic judgment and the same fearful audacity. It takes bravery and faith, but it makes for a better world.

NOTE

1. V. O. Key, *Southern Politics in State and Nation* (Cambridge, MA: Harvard University Press, 1949), 310.

CLAY RISEN

Untrod Ground

Civil War History Today

I**S THERE ANY** better trod topic in American history than the Civil War? In 2009 the historian James M. McPherson, in his foreword to the *Library of Congress Civil War Desk Reference*, estimated that between fifty thousand and seventy thousand books and monographs about the conflict had appeared since its conclusion.[1] In 2021, nearly six years past the end of the war's sesquicentennial, that number is undoubtedly much higher. There are the dozens of Civil War journals and magazines, hundreds of conferences, thousands of lectures. It's enough to make a book browser look upon the latest Ulysses S. Grant biography and despair.

Yet the books keep coming, and somehow, they keep having something new to say. It is the nature of history writing, and especially history writing about this seminal American story: if the war, as Robert Penn Warren wrote, "draws us as an oracle, darkly unriddled and portentous of our personal and our national fate," then its insights will by necessity change as America itself changes.[2] The questions that a multiracial, globalized nation asks of its history in 2021 are very different from those asked by the same country fifty years prior, when it was a segregated superpower locked in a nuclear-tipped cold war.

During the 1950s, a time of often repressive national consensus, the questions revolved around proving that the war could have been avoided, the better to demonstrate that all was fine with America and always had been, save for the odd hiccup. A few decades later, the country had shifted, and so had the questions: the war was inevitable because conflict, not consensus, was endemic to the American political psyche—a view that came naturally to the '60s generation, and even more so to their children in the early twenty-first century, when polarization became the defining quality of American politics and society. And so we have books like Joanne B. Freeman's *The Field of Blood: Violence in Congress and the Road to Civil War* (2018) and Andrew Delbanco's *The War Before the War: Fugitive Slaves and the Struggle for America's*

Soul from the Revolution to the Civil War (2018), both of which see the Civil War as the nearly inevitable consequence of America's founding paradox as a nation built on both freedom and slavery.

Traveling alongside these assessments about the war's roots are historians asking wholly new questions about the conflict through the lens of enslaved people and women and culture, things that their elders ignored but that the new, post–civil rights America made necessary to explore. Most notable among these works are Drew Gilpin Faust's *This Republic of Suffering: Death and the American Civil War* (2008) and Stephanie McCurry's *Women's War: Fighting and Surviving the American Civil War* (2015).

In asking different questions, historians not only get different answers, but they discover new evidence that feeds back on, and obliterates, received truths. Few historians in the 1950s cared to ask what women thought and did during the war; over the subsequent half century, new questions have led historians to examine previously overlooked sources, which in turn have shed new light on conventional wisdom about all facets of the war. Women, we now know, not only played important roles on the battlefront, but through their positions as informal political advisers and activists, they helped shape the course of the war on the home front as well.

What sort of questions are historians asking today? If a consensus exists, it is that there is no consensus—if it's not quite "anything goes," it's certainly a much more permissive, wide-ranging field of inquiry than before. The radical, insurgent perspective has become the establishment.

Material culture and mass media are frequent subjects. In the *New York Times*'s Disunion series, we published young scholars writing on Civil War music, Civil War humor, and Civil War literature, all of which points to further investigation in the coming years. Recent books reflect that same instinct, like Jonathan W. White's *Midnight in America: Darkness, Sleep, and Dreams during the Civil War* (2019). Regional experiences are also of new interest—the war in the Appalachians, or the Carolina coast, for example. That old chestnut about the Civil War pitting "brother against brother" is once again at the front of scholarly minds as historians examine how communities along the North–South border navigated the violence of divided loyalties.

Though the *New York Times*'s 1619 Project is not about the Civil War per se, it raises questions about the centrality of slavery to the American experience and critiques the belief that American history is one of progress toward greater equality led by white male Americans. Accompanying the project, at least in spirit, are books that put the Black experience at the heart of the abolitionist and Civil War narrative, like Matthew Harper's *The End of Days: African American Religion and Politics in the Age of Emancipation* (2016), and how African Americans led their own struggle for freedom, like Manisha Sinha's *The Slave's Cause* (2016), David W. Blight's *Frederick Douglass: Prophet of Freedom* (2018), and W. Caleb McDaniel's *Sweet Taste of Liberty: A True Story of Slavery and Restitution in America* (2019), the latter two of which won the Pulitzer Prize.

There is also a movement to put the Civil War in an international context. In part this involves a deeper investigation into the war's diplomatic aspects, the view from London and Paris, as it were, embodied most recently in Amanda Foreman's *A World on Fire: Britain's Crucial Role in the American Civil War* (2010). This is hardly new ground: Frank L. Owsley Sr. wrote *King Cotton Diplomacy: Foreign Relations of the Confederate States of America* (1931), still often considered the standard text on Civil War foreign policy, in 1931. But the staying power of that book, written by an avowed, if erudite, racist, demonstrates why a book like Foreman's—and, hopefully, others to follow— is so needed.

Most significantly, scholars have clarified how deeply the Haitian revolution resonated throughout antebellum southern society.[3] The fear that a slave population could rise up and defeat a white master class—a fear underscored by the occasional domestic slave revolt—made southern whites increasingly paranoid throughout the first half of the nineteenth century, to the point that any possible challenge to their social structure became a life-or-death threat. At the same time, they pushed endlessly for any avenue for expansion of slave-owning territory: the annexation of Texas, the Mexican War, the invasion of Nicaragua by *filibusteros*. Indeed, it is impossible to understand the southern fear of Republican power—culminating in Lincoln's election—without understanding this international context.

This is hardly unique to Civil War history. Americans, including American historians, have long tended to see the country's history in isolation, with any relationship to the outside world relegated to subdisciplines like diplomatic history. But that has started to change. In recent decades scholars have insisted that the United States, from its earliest colonial moments, was part of a transatlantic world, both influencing and influenced by events in Europe.

Andre Fleche, a young professor and a contributor to Disunion, has written extensively on the causal and thematic connections between the revolutionary spirit of mid-nineteenth-century Europe and the onset of the Civil War. Kenneth Weisbrode noted in a 2011 piece for Disunion that the Civil War, when seen alongside Prussia's wars of the late 1840s to the early 1870s, represents a new, centralizing, and modernizing tendency in North Atlantic history—no wonder Otto von Bismarck said he looked to Abraham Lincoln for inspiration.[4] Likewise, Don H. Doyle, in his articles for Disunion and his book *Nations Divided: America, Italy, and the Southern Question* (2012), has shown how the American Civil War was just one part of a nineteenth-century struggle between democracy and repression across the Western world.[5] At the same time, the American Civil War, though horrible, was a food fight in comparison with the Chinese civil war (1850–1864)—concerns over which, some historians now claim, was the decisive reason Britain ultimately stayed neutral in the American conflict. All politics is local, but all history is global.

Thanks to improvements in information technology, historians can now ask questions that they never thought possible to answer. Scholars at the University of Richmond have shoveled thousands of Civil War–era pages from the *Richmond Dispatch* into a database, which they can sift through to find once-hidden patterns. For instance, they found that notices for runaway slaves tended to spike after Union victories, hinting strongly that slaves were not only well aware of the course of the war but willing to act on the news they received—conclusions that undercut conventional assumptions about slaves as passive, uninformed pawns in a white man's war.[6]

Amazingly, there are wide swaths of Civil War history that remain poorly covered. Southern history, despite a few recent, groundbreaking works like Stephanie McCurry's *Confederate Reckoning* (2010), is woefully underappreciated. It is a minefield, one that scholars may not want to enter: taking the Confederate States of America seriously as an institution and the South seriously as a political culture may be seen as giving them credibility at a time when public displays of southern pride and the Confederate battle flag are rightly considered expressions of white supremacy.

There is also much work to be done on the American West during the war. We tend to see the Civil War and the later settlement of the West as two discrete stories. But they weren't: conflicts with Native Americans were frequent during the Civil War, most notably the Dakota War of 1862. Moreover, the war forced many Native American tribes to take sides, choices that reverberated through the rest of the century. Attitudes toward violence and power that were forged during the war helped ease qualms about massacring Native Americans later, a point brought home in recent books like Megan Kate Nelson's *The Three-Cornered War* (2020), Andrew E. Masich's *Civil War in the Southwest Borderlands, 1861–1867* (2017), Heather Cox Richardson's *West from Appomattox* (2017), and T. J. Jackson Lears's *Rebirth of a Nation* (2009).

When we began publishing Disunion in November 2010, we weren't sure how popular the series would be, or how much new there would be to say, at least to a general audience. Not only has the series been immensely popular, but we've also been impressed by the depth and breadth of new perspectives coming from established and rising scholars, both inside and outside the university gates. While we like to think we're publishing the best of what's available, we also hope that the series inspires even younger scholars and writers to enter Civil War history. The field remains wide open.

NOTES

1. James M. McPherson, *The Library of Congress Civil War Desk Reference* (New York: Random House, 2009), xix–xx.

2. Robert Penn Warren, *The Legacy of the Civil War* (Lincoln: Bison Books, reprinted in 1998), 102.

3. See, for example, Matthew Calvin, *Toussaint Louverture and the American Civil War: The Promise and Peril of a Second Haitian Revolution* (Philadelphia: University of Pennsylvania Press, 2010) and Tim Matthewson, *A Proslavery Foreign Policy: Haitian–American Relations During the Early Republic* (Westport: Praeger, 2003).

4. Kenneth Weisbrode, "Why Bismarck Loved Lincoln," *New York Times*, Oct. 2, 2011, https://opinionator.blogs.nytimes.com/2011/10/02/why-bismarck-loved-lincoln/.

5. Don Doyle, "Vive L'Union," *New York Times*, Oct. 16, 2001, https://opinionator.blogs.nytimes.com/2011/10/16/vive-lunion/; "Roma o Morte!" *New York Times*, Oct. 4, 2012, https://opinionator.blogs.nytimes.com/2012/10/04/roma-o-morte/; and "How the Civil War Changed the World," *New York Times*, May 19, 2015, https://opinionator.blogs.nytimes.com/2015/05/19/how-the-civil-war-changed-the-world/.

6. See "Hidden Patterns of the Civil War" at the Digital Scholarship Lab, University of Richmond, http://americanpast.org/civilwar/vizemanccite.html.

JOHN P. DUNN

King Cotton, the Khedive, and the American Civil War

ALTHOUGH ABOUT AS far away from the American South as allowed by Earth's geography, Egypt was tremendously impacted by the American Civil War. Diplomats from the North and South jockeyed for influence in Egypt; Egypt's Khedive Sa'id contributed soldiers for the concurrent French intervention in Mexico while John Suratt, one of the Lincoln conspirators, was apprehended at Alexandria. Of course, these would all be footnotes in our history books save for the story of cotton. Cotton interweaves the story of southern plantations, English cotton mills, and Egyptian *fellahine* (small farmers) throughout the nineteenth century.

Although Ancient Egyptians used cotton for clothing, tents, and to wrap mummies, and Medieval Egyptians exported enough to create a name for the product—via the Arabic *qutn* (قطن), which morphed into the Spanish *algodón*, then the English cotton—this connection was not in one direction only. Several times in the nineteenth century, Egypt and the American South impacted each other's cotton industry. It all started with a meeting between Louis Jumel and Muhammad Ali. The former was connected to the French cotton industry; the latter ruled Egypt from 1805 until 1848.

Muhammad Ali was a talented Albanian adventurer who wanted to dramatically alter the land of the Nile via his *nizam al-jadid*, or "new organization." This transformation called for major improvements in Egypt's political, educational, economic, and military systems. Muhammad Ali combined crafty politics, tremendous willpower, and a splash of luck, but he also understood he'd require a significant cash flow for it to work.

Enter Louis Jumel (1785–1823), an entrepreneur with ties to the French cotton industry. Jumel saw Egypt as an excellent supplier for French mills. Not, however, with the plants currently growing along the Nile. Instead, Jumel wanted to import both American seeds from Georgia and seeds from Peru to create a hybrid of Sea Island and

Peruvian cotton. He sold this idea to Muhammad Ali in 1819 and, within a few years, was planting fields and supervising mills.

This was no small venture, as Muhammad Ali had six hundred thousand acres of prime agricultural land at his disposal and millions of fellahine, whose status was somewhat similar to contemporary Russian serfs. They worked the land for very little compensation, were sent to the mills, or conscripted into Egypt's armed forces. Cotton required more than rainwater, and as a result, a series of canals and irrigation channels were crisscrossing northern Egypt by the 1830s. With land, fellahine, and water, Egypt was set to produce large quantities of cotton for export. And cash flowed back to fund Muhammad Ali's new organization.

Jumel's American hybrid was the start of what we today call long staple Egyptian cotton. It had an extralong staple, the fluffy lint inside the boll, sometimes up to one and a half inches. Its length and nature allowed a very high thread count, making it possible to convert this cotton into excellent thread, durable bedsheets, or very soft underwear.

By 1835, thirty mills, employing twelve thousand workers, produced cotton products both for home consumption and export. Historian Jason Thompson described this venture as "the most efficient exploitation of the resources of Egypt since Roman times." Muhammad Ali seemed ready to spread his new organization throughout the Middle East. Although appointed *wali*, or governor, by the Ottoman sultan, Muhammad Ali had rapidly detached Egypt from the empire. By the 1820s, he was the de facto ruler, and a decade later, powerful enough to challenge the sultan's authority throughout the Middle East.

These moves were stopped by British intervention, mainly to buttress the Ottoman Empire, but also partially to protect English cotton mills. Facing a formidable alliance of European great powers, Muhammad Ali backed down, and his cotton mills, without protection from established European competition, closed in the 1840s. Egypt reverted to its role as exporter of raw materials. It was not until the outbreak of the American Civil War that Egypt's cotton economy soared under Muhammad Ali's successors: Sa'id, his youngest son (1854–1863), and Isma'il, his grandson (1863–1879).

As historian Edward Earle puts it, "one cannot study the history of Egypt during the last half of the nineteenth century, without being profoundly impressed by the importance of the American Civil War in the making of modern Egypt." Khedive Sa'id recognized the US Civil War could be long, and the massive Federal Navy would conduct a successful blockade. Doing so would dethrone "King Cotton," America's number one export before 1861. The "king" was tremendously valuable, a crop, which, in 1859, produced $161 million, or 48 percent of the total value of US products sold overseas. Despite daring blockade-runners, and even Yankee businessmen who colluded to sneak southern cotton to northern mills, the blockade worked as Sa'id expected—it left most southern cotton at home.

Egypt, on the other hand, was positioned to pick up the slack, and there was a lot of slack in 1861. With the introduction of power looms and cotton gins in the eighteenth century, Europeans had developed a major need for raw cotton. Who would supply these mills during the Civil War? The answer: A little from India, Brazil, and Central Asia, but mainly Egypt.

Sa'id started the ball rolling by reducing the export duty to .01 percent, correctly assuming he'd still reap a fortune from the increased demand. This encouraged big landowners to plant more cotton, allowing Egypt to double its production. According to an 1864 *New York Times* article, this was still not enough, and the price of Egyptian cotton rose dramatically. In 1859, when King Cotton still ruled, Egyptian cotton brought $12 per *kantar* (about 99 pounds). By 1864, it sold for $45 per kantar. Even the fellahine were making money.

So was Sa'id's successor Isma' il, called "the Magnificent" by European admirers, "the Builder," by more neutral Egyptians, or "Pimp Pasha" by enemies who claimed his tax system was so extensive that even prostitutes provided government revenues. Entitled Khedive, or "Great Master," Isma'il came to power at the height of the US Civil War and Egypt's cotton boom. He already had extensive experience successfully running the family plantations and, like his grandfather, had big plans for Egypt, and with a steady cash flow, the means to start them.

Cotton revenues helped Isma'il complete the Suez Canal; construct the first opera house in the Middle East, for which Verdi wrote *Aida* and which the French empress attended; dredge harbors; lay telegraph lines; and dream of reconstructing Muhammad Ali's empire. Unlike his grandfather, Isma'il focused on Africa rather than Syria, but this was an equally impressive imperial venture, requiring lots of firepower and military muscle, again connecting Egypt and America.

Army modernization was one of Isma'il's many projects, and who better to help out than officers with experience from the world's most recent struggle? Between 1869 and 1879, upward of fifty ex-Confederate and Union officers helped create an Egyptian general staff. Led by Charles P. Stone, this contingent of Civil War veterans was far from perfect. Some were excellent; a few were drunkards or talentless. Yet, if not "the best money could buy," they did get along well, for as one put it, "There is no North or South here."

Another Civil War spin-off was Isma'il's decision to purchase millions of dollars' worth of American weapons. US manufacturers eagerly sought new markets and benefitted from the Egyptian perception that US Civil War needs created the best designs. Thus, Remington rifles, Gatling guns, arms factories, and ammunition all figured in lucrative contracts to US companies.

Isma'il, "the Spender," could no longer use cotton to support these schemes. It was still desirable but had dropped to $19.50 per kantar by 1870. Loans and bond sales temporarily made up the difference until European bankers said "no more." Finally, in 1875, to fund his US Civil War veterans on an imperial adventure into Ethiopia, Isma'il sold off his share of the Suez Canal. Purchase by the British started all kinds of challenges for the end of Isma'il's reign and connects us again to cotton, with threads stretching from Egypt to America.

Egypt experienced considerable political turmoil between 1878 and 1882. When the turmoil was over, a British army occupied the Land of the Nile, and London, either directly or through surrogates, pulled most of the political strings until 1946. Members of the Muhammad Ali dynasty kept their throne and a share of what power the British allowed, until 1952. These were not good years for Egyptian nationalists who saw their land occupied by outsiders.

Simultaneously, Egypt faced a financial challenge—paying off the debts of Khedive Isma'il. Frugal budgets and more cotton helped accomplish this goal. Every March through April, the fellahine planted cotton; they then picked the bolls in October, with a second picking in January, after which the plant was uprooted for use as fuel. Next March, repeat, then rotate with a cereal crop.

Long staple Egyptian cotton still held a good market share, and by 1913, it accounted for 6.5 percent of the world's production by weight but 10 percent by value. The towels and bed linens you see promoted everywhere today, which read "made from 100% Egyptian cotton," started when early twentieth-century manufacturers recognized the very high thread count not only provided durability but also an attractive sheen and softness.

Cotton mills in the American South were importing Egyptian cotton at the turn of the last century. If you wanted superior yarn, thread, socks, or undergarments, Egyptian cotton trumped the homegrown. It also blended well with silk and was better at holding color. These advantages encouraged the Department of Agriculture to import Egyptian cotton seeds and establish experimental farms in the American Southwest. With a similar climate to Egypt's, parts of Texas, Arizona, New Mexico, and California began to produce "Egyptian cotton." Cheap water helped convert these states into major cotton producers during the twentieth century. Today Texas and California lead the United States in cotton production, and although King Cotton has long been dethroned, cotton production generates considerable income across the South.

Egypt remains a player in the world cotton market but faces many challenges today. Overthrowing Muhammad Ali's dynasty in 1952, a military oligarchy with populist leanings broke up the big estates, providing the fellahine with farms. Undercapitalized, these small-scale cotton producers were hard-pressed to embrace technology that enhanced cotton production elsewhere. At the same time, the new regime imported

Soviet technical and economic forms, producing rather cumbersome mills that could not compete on the world market. When new oligarchs embraced capitalism in the 1970s, these mills became even less useful. Still, by marketing the long staple brand created by the partnership of Muhammad Ali and Louis Jumel, Egypt holds a niche with its high-grade lint. Who is to say that some new partnership will not revitalize the Nile Valley?

SUGGESTIONS FOR FURTHER READING

Sven Beckert, *Empire of Cotton: A Global History* (New York: Vintage, 2014).

Edward Mead Earle, "Egyptian Cotton and the American Civil War," *Political Science Quarterly* 41, no. 4 (1926): 520–545.

William B. Hesseltine and Hazel C. Wolf, *The Blue and the Gray on the Nile* (Chicago: University of Chicago Press, 1961).

Walaa Hussein, "Is There an Egyptian Cotton Conspiracy," *Al-Monitor*, March 20, 2015, http://www.al-monitor.com/pulse/originals/2015/03/egypt-cotton-production-increase -decrease-textile.html.

David G. Surdam, "King Cotton: Monarch or Pretender? The State of the Market for Raw Cotton on the Eve of the American Civil War," *Economic History Review* 51, no. 1 (1998): 113–132.

KAREN L. COX

It Was Always the River

Natchez on the Mississippi

OMETIME IN 2015, as I was sitting in the visitors' center in Natchez, Mississippi, watching one of those introductory films developed for tourists, I first heard the words: "It was always the river." They were spoken softly by a woman as the sun's rays reflected hues of yellow and orange on the Mississippi River. Whether it was her intention, the woman whose voice accompanied that image had made a telling statement about the river's place in the lives of Natchezeans, past and present, and it has echoed in my mind ever since.

My many visits to Natchez prior to that time had been for a book I was writing. I had been traveling there since 2012 to get to know the town and its environs and to conduct research about a murder that took place there in 1932. The crime, which made headlines nationwide and was known locally as the Goat Castle murder, nearly eclipsed the great publicity surrounding the first pilgrimage to antebellum homes earlier that spring. Researching and writing that book, which became *Goat Castle: A True Story of Murder, Race, and the Gothic South* (2017), repeatedly brought me back to this historic town that hugs the bluffs overlooking the Mississippi River.

The river is the town's raison d'être.

Natchez is the oldest settlement on the lower half of the Mississippi River and earned its name from the area's original inhabitants, the Natchez Indians. Over time, Natchez became home to the French (who established Fort Rosalie in 1716), the English (following the Seven Years' War with England, the fort was ceded to the British in 1763), the Spanish (from 1779 to 1798, during which time Natchez began to take shape as a city laid out in the common grid pattern under territorial governor Manuel Gayoso de Lemos), and finally the Americans in 1798, when Natchez came under the control of the US government.

The town has had its fair share of famous visitors throughout its history. When it was the capital of the Mississippi Territory, former vice president Aaron Burr was arrested near Natchez for conspiring to create a separate nation, though he was released and later acquitted of charges of treason. Two decades later, the American naturalist John James Audubon spent a few months in Natchez painting birds; he also enrolled his sons at nearby Jefferson Academy, a military school for young boys. P. T. Barnum brought the Swedish singing sensation Jenny Lind to Natchez in 1851, where she performed to a sellout crowd, as she had done in cities across the United States.

The river, and the rich lands it fed, brought northern investors from New York, Pennsylvania, and Massachusetts, who took advantage of the antebellum cotton boom as well as the nation's institution of slavery. Just like their southern counterparts, these Northerners helped to create the demand for slave labor that resulted in the sale and forced relocation of between 750,000 and one million men, women, and children from states in the Upper South to the Deep South states of Mississippi and Louisiana. While a majority of those enslaved were sold in the city of New Orleans, thousands were sent upriver to Natchez, where they were sold at the slave-trading post known as the Forks of the Road.

Military control of the Mississippi River has always been strategically important, but it was particularly so during the Civil War. Once General Ulysses Grant's troops took control of the town of Vicksburg after a weeks-long siege, Federal troops went farther south, to Natchez, where in August 1863 they occupied the town and placed Black soldiers on patrol, shocking white Natchezeans. Those same soldiers, some of them former slaves, also took pleasure in destroying the slave pens at the Forks of the Road, which signaled the end of the institution of chattel slavery.

The river was, for all intents and purposes, an important highway of travel and trade in the nineteenth century. As Mark Twain, himself a steamboat pilot on the Mississippi, explained: "The river's earliest commerce was in great barges—keelboats, broadhorns. They floated and sailed from the upper rivers to New Orleans, changed cargoes there, and were tediously warped and poled back by hand. A voyage down and back sometimes occupied nine months."

With that commerce came some unsavory characters who helped shape the bad reputation of the land below Natchez's bluffs. "It gave employment to hordes of rough and hardy men," wrote Twain, "rude, uneducated, brave, suffering terrific hardships with sailor-like stoicism; heavy drinkers, coarse frolickers in moral sties like the Natchez-under-the-hill of that day, heavy fighters, reckless fellows, every one, elephantinely jolly, foul-witted, profane; prodigal of their money, bankrupt at the end of the trip, fond of barbaric finery, prodigious braggarts; yet, in the main, honest, trustworthy, faithful to promises and duty, and often picturesquely magnanimous."[1]

As the nineteenth century gave way to the twentieth, Natchez seemed to be bypassed by modernity. Trains replaced steamboats, and while the Illinois Central Railroad made a stop in Natchez, the river traffic nearly dried up. There was no bridge across the Mississippi until 1940, so for almost half of the twentieth century, travelers to Natchez from points west had to be ferried across from the town of Vidalia, Louisiana.

And yet in the midst of the Great Depression, travelers did venture to Natchez despite its isolation—crossing by ferry over the river to see its magnificent antebellum mansions, which made the town synonymous with Old South grandeur. This tour of antebellum homes, known as the Natchez Pilgrimage, still draws tourists to this day. And the river has once again become home to steamboat replicas that bring tourists by the thousands every year.

As someone who has made repeated treks to Natchez, I am always drawn to the river. Like Frederick Law Olmstead before me, who visited in 1852, I have sought out its bluffs to get the splendid view of this force of nature. As he noted, "the grand feature of Natchez is the bluff, terminating in an abrupt precipitous bank over the river." And while there is now a river walk and fence to protect people from tumbling over the "precipitous bank," it remains the place I venture to most frequently. The swift moving waters and the amazing sunsets over and beyond Louisiana continues to fascinate and thrill me. I've seen sunsets in blue and yellow, pink and blue, golden yellow, and one evening there was a sunset of fiery orange that nearly took my breath away. I have walked along the bluffs numerous times and have never been disappointed with what nature has produced.

Yet my fascination with the land and sky is tempered by my knowledge of America's history of slavery because there, under those same sunsets were thousands of acres given to planting cotton, and where the human chattel of the domestic slave trade—men, women, and children—provided the free labor that made millionaires of men in the lower Mississippi Valley, which included Natchez.

Understanding this doesn't distract from the river's historical significance or the place it has in the minds and memories of Natchezeans, which is why those words "it was always the river" still resonate.

NOTE

1. *Life on the Mississippi* (Boston: James R. Osgood, 1883), 41.

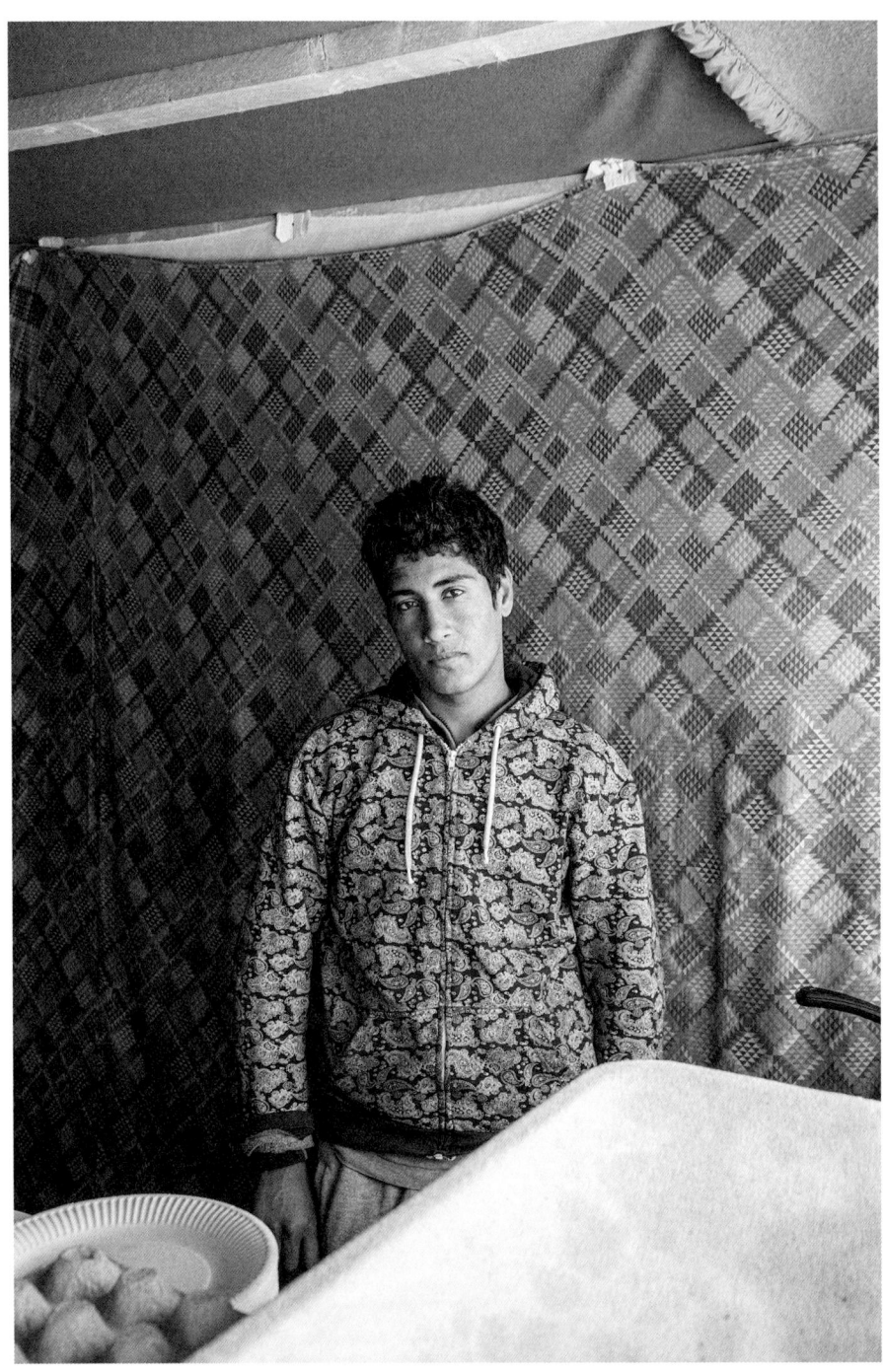

Lewis Watts, Untitled, Refugee camp in Calais, France, 2015, courtesy of the artist

HOMELANDS

MICHAEL MALONE

Landscapes of the Imagination

Writing the South

"The woods are full of regional writers and it is the horror
of every serious Southern writer that he will become one."
—Flannery O'Connor

J ACK KEROUAC told us, "Nobody'll ever know America completely because nobody ever knew Gatsby, I guess."[1] But it was not while living at home in America that F. Scott Fitzgerald wrote that most American of novels, *The Great Gatsby*. Instead, he was wandering unrooted among the rich in Paris and the French Riviera (like some disenchanted hero of a trite tale told by Jay Gatsby himself). Had Fitzgerald not been obliged to rely on transatlantic cables to communicate with his editor, Maxwell Perkins, in New York about *Gatsby*, it's possible he would have succeeded—he tried—in persuading Perkins once again to change the novel's title, this time to *Under the Red, White and Blue*, a declaration that *Gatsby* distills our national mythology. As for the Riviera, it became the setting for the novel that he finally managed to write nine years later while living in Baltimore: *Tender Is the Night*.

The map of Fitzgerald's compositions shows a pattern—he moves away, turns back, and looks: at St. Paul, Minnesota; at Princeton; at Long Island; at the Riviera. In the end, he stopped at the edge of the West, in Hollywood, from which there was nowhere else to go. And he said just that in the almost-finished *The Last Tycoon*. Exile in Hollywood gave him that last novel.

Landscape is an invaluable gift to a writer. But distance from that landscape can also open doors to roads otherwise never taken, and so make "all the difference." Speaking of her forced departure from Chile, novelist Isabel Allende explained to an interviewer, "I started my first novel ... because I was living in exile in Venezuela and my grandfather was dying in Chile. And I could not return to be with him, so I started a letter for him that turned into *The House of the Spirits*."[2] Would her novel have been different had Allende never left Chile? Or is she implying that perhaps it never would have been written?

I've always wanted to go visit that local habitation and dwelling place in which a novelist created a work I love. In my travels to pay calls on fellow American writers, I've visited hundreds of sites, as varied as the log cabin where Twain came up with "The Jumping Frog of Calaveras County" to the elegant mansion in the Berkshires, The Mount, where Edith Wharton wrote from her bed. Abroad, I'm always paying a call on writers' homes, schools, bars, theaters, graves.

Sometimes writers live out their lives in the settings of the fictions they write. In an English village, Jane Austen wrote novels that take place right there "at home," in, as it were, her own drawing room, just outside her windows, and up the High Street in just such an English village as her imagined one.

Other writers are looking at home from a place far away, as Isak Dinesen moved out of Africa before she wrote *Out of Africa*. We can wonder, would James Joyce have described the Dublin streets of *Ulysses* differently had he been still living in that city, where the entirely Irish June 16 that we now know as Bloomsday, took place? Might he instead, for example, have set Bloomsday in the present, at the start of the 1920s, rather than in the past (1904)? Might he have taken us into other pubs, let us hear other voices? Through his long exile (Trieste, Zurich, and Paris), the Irish author certainly didn't expect any other dwelling place ever to provide the core setting for his fiction: "For myself, I always write about Dublin, because if I can get to the heart of Dublin I can get to the heart of all the cities of the world. In the particular is contained the universal."[3]

That "particular" changes from writer to writer; often for the same writer, it changes from book to book. Of a trilogy of mine called the Hillston novels, all three featuring the same characters and set in the North Carolina Piedmont, I wrote *Uncivil Seasons* in Connecticut, *Time's Witness* in Philadelphia, and I began *First Lady* in London and finished it in Hillsborough, a small southern town very much like the one where the novels take place.

The first novel, *Uncivil Seasons,* is narrated by Justin Savile V, very much an insider in his southern community. He begins his tale with a communal "We."

Two things don't happen very often in Hillston, North Carolina. We don't get much snow and we hardly ever murder one another. Suicide is more our style; we're a quiet college town and our lives are sheltered by old trees.

The second book, *Time's Witness* is a novel about white nationalism and the racial use of the death penalty. It is narrated by Justin's close friend, Cuddy Mangum—a brainy, highly moral and politically savvy outsider from the wrong side of town—who has just surprised Justin by being appointed chief of police, and so, Justin's boss.

The third book, *First Lady*, returns to Savile as the narrator. It opens:

I go riding in the mornings on a horse named Manassas. I ride the old bridle path that runs behind the big summerhouses at Pine Hills Lake. The lake is just outside Hillston, North Carolina, where my family has always lived. My family's circle is wide. My circle is this narrow red clay track around the lake.

Is there a discernible difference in how I heard Justin's voice in the first book, when I sat in a cold winter's room beside a New England salt marsh and how I heard his voice many years later in a summer's London flat? I don't think so.

On the other hand, if you ask me whether I would have written any one of those three novels had I not been raised in the South's Piedmont, the answer would be no, absolutely not. For the North Carolina Piedmont, my childhood home, has always been in fiction my "particular," my Hannibal, Missouri, my Yoknapatawpha, my home.

"My particular" for authors can mean any of a number of different fiction places, of different *kinds* of fictional places. A place never seen (or seeable) except in the imagination (Jules Verne never flew to Mars or traveled twenty thousand leagues under the sea). Lawrence Thornton, a professor in California, wrote *Imagining Argentina* in 1991 without ever having personally experienced the Dirty War of the 1970s in Buenos Aires. But he imagined it with such extraordinary clarity that the book won the PEN/Hemingway Award. (I served on that committee, and I remember my surprise at first learning that Thornton had done exactly what his title declares: He had *imagined* Argentina).

However, it is more probable that a writer in search of a setting will pick if not her or his current home, then a landscape once personally known, revisited in the writer's imagination, often a place long left behind but foundational. Present life can be a pale imitation of those dreamed pasts of our childhoods and our youths, when our senses were more permeable and our spongy minds soaked in sharp ardent memories and kept them in our memories, unfaded. Willa Cather's family moved to Red Cloud, Nebraska when she was nine years old, and she left behind that flat, dusty town at fifteen. But her fictional landscape remained Red Cloud, in novel after novel, with its endlessly rolling waves of prairie, where "the grass was the country, as the water is the sea." Red Cloud is the land Cather was talking about when she advised Eudora Welty that writers must let their fiction grow out of "the land beneath their feet."

America is so big a country that all our writers could be called regional writers, deeply distinct from one another. New England poets. New York playwrights. Southern novelists. But we're a restless country too. We won't stay put, confined by region. We're always telling each other to go West, to fly to the moon, to "move on." We tend not to die in the same place we were born. We are likely to agree that everybody, as Sinclair Lewis pointed out, "needs a hometown to get away from." (Some years ago,

I paid a visit to Lewis's hometown, Sauk Centre, Minnesota, and happened to arrive when there was a banner over Main Street that declared that the town merchants were in the middle of their annual Sinclair Lewis Days celebration. The author of *Babbitt* would have gotten a kick out of their boosterism.)

But if there is any part of this country where writers do tend to stay put—both in how they define themselves as writers and in how they choose the subject matter of their fiction—it's the South. That's why legend has it that after only a few weeks in Hollywood, William Faulkner asked the movie studio who'd employed him, "Mind if I work at home?" And when the studio said "Sure," Faulkner packed up and returned to Mississippi. That's the legend. The reality is that Faulkner hung around film studio Dream Factories for extended stays in the '30s, '40s, and '50s, drinking at the Garden of Allah, having an affair with a secretary, hunting with Howard Hawks, and working on *Mildred Pierce* and *The Big Sleep*. But the legend tells us that a southern writer went home to Mississippi because a southern writer needs to be in his Yoknapatawpha, his "little postage stamp of native soil." As they say in *The Man Who Shot Liberty Valance*, between the fact and the legend, always print the legend. For southerners, the myth is the South.

I am often introduced as a southern writer, although I lived in the Northeast most of my adult life, and as a result the majority of my novels were composed above the Mason–Dixon Line. But while I never like to see my novels separated by genre (bookstores may put *Handling Sin* in a "Literature" shelf, *Time's Witness* in "Mystery"), I never mind finding myself on a shelf of "Southern Writers." Why? Because I believe that designation speaks to something real. Did you ever hear anybody introduced as "a northern writer"? So is there something different about our native southern soil, that if we do leave home, we carry it with us like the earth in a vampire's coffin? I think so. Because to be southern is still to see from a slant, from a minority position, from the outsider point of view. Ever hear anyone speak of a wonderful "male" poet or a great "white" actress? It doesn't occur to the Insiders that they need to specify a distinction from some Other. Insiders have been led to believe they are the All. Most southerners know there's something else, and that if not accepted as the baseline, it's useful as a contrast.

My first three novels were not even set in the South, but they all had expatriate southerners among their characters, individuals slightly apart from the others, people looking at things from a tilt, sometimes with a winked eye. I'm reminded that I drew complete detailed maps for the two fictional towns I'd imagined as the settings of those early novels: one for Floren Park in *The Delectable Mountains*, a version of Estes Park, Colorado, where I'd spent a summer in a stock company; and one for *Dingley Falls*, influenced by my visit to Washington Depot in the Litchfield Hills of Connecticut. The maps of those imaginary towns appear as the inside covers of the published novels. The critic Malcolm Cowley, who then lived in western Connecticut, told me Dingley Falls was the most southern town he'd ever seen plunked down in a Connecticut novel.

I never drew a map of any southern town in my fiction. Maybe that's because I didn't need to.

For years now I have told and retold the story of how in my early twenties, I drove all the way from North Carolina to Jackson, Mississippi, to let Eudora Welty know how much I admired her work. She still lived in the house in which she'd grown up, and if you knew someone from Jackson, you could learn its address. But parked across the street from her home, I lost my nerve in the end. I just sat in my car for hours, then drove off to Oxford, Mississippi, to visit Faulkner's grave. There were wilted flowers and a bottle of whiskey leaning on his tombstone, gifts from admirers. We had a long lopsided conversation.

A decade later, I met Eudora Welty at a reading at Yale University. And then more than another decade later, I talked with her in the lobby of the Algonquin Hotel. I told her then that story of my travel to her home in Jackson so long ago.

She said, "Honey, was that you? I almost called the police on you!" It pleased her that I'd published three novels, but when I described them—*Painting the Roses Red* is set in California and in Cambridge; *Delectable Mountains* in Colorado; *Dingley Falls* in Connecticut—her mouth lifted in that smile of hers. "All those c's! Guess what? You're just sneaking up on Carolina."

It was perhaps the most resonant remark anyone ever made to me as a young writer. Back in that town by the New England salt marsh where I was then living, I imagined North Carolina. And I've kept doing that. In my fiction, time and again I come back to that red clay Piedmont country that is the landscape of my imagination. Years later, for reasons beyond my own work, my wife and I moved to that very region when she accepted a position as chair of Duke's English Department. She'd never lived in the South and found it both alien and fascinating: "I feel like I've moved inside one of your novels. . . . There goes Cuddy Mangum by in his police car. There're all the crazy Hayes family in *Handling Sin*. . . . I thought it was just you, but everybody down here acts like you."

At the same time that the South is somehow the "outside," the defeated, after all, by a stronger force, the South is the center for a southern writer. To place oneself there is to put oneself at a center of meaning, often dark, violent, tragic meaning. It is to align the individual self to a social self that is definable, relatable, historic and mythic, in some ways damned, in some ways redemptive. In the South, you don't need to question whether you can repeat the past or not. Of course you can! What you have to learn is how not to do it.

You carry the southern past with you, in your family, in the South's history and in some ways most deeply in its storytelling fictions. The relationship between the two narrators of my Hillston novels, Justin B. Savile V and Cuddy Mangum, owes as much to Twain's Tom Sawyer and Huck Finn as to my growing up in the Piedmont.

Some years back, I moderated two separate panels at the Southern Festival of Books in Nashville. One of them gathered writers from the North who were then living in the South; the other brought together writers from the South then living in the North. After the panels finished, the northerner participants sat around discussing their belief that there had been no real reason they should ever have been on such a panel together. Meanwhile, the southerners took off together in a hired van for trips to the Parthenon and Tootsie's Orchid Lounge.

My generation of southern writers saw themselves on rafts in a great flotilla floating down the same river. We'd been warned to believe both that you can't go home again (so Thomas Wolfe had advised, melancholy and relieved) and at the same time that you can never escape from home in the first place. Often southerners don't ever leave home at all. Eudora Welty and Flannery O'Connor never did. "Southern writers are stuck with the South, and it's a good thing to be stuck with," argued O'Connor, from the farmhouse Andalusia in Milledgeville, Georgia, where she lived with her mother. Of some new group of artful writers, she quipped, "You know what's the matter with them? They're not *frum* anywhere."[4]

Of course many southern writers do leave home and never come back. But mostly they take the South with them, as did Mark Twain, when he wrote his southern books in Hartford, Connecticut; Elmira, New York; London, England. A writer can't get away from what lies at the heart of southern fiction—it's always about "space and race," as the plot of our foundational text, *Huckleberry Finn*, has been described. In that novel, Huck and Jim keep trying to head north up the Mississippi, to get away from the South. But in the end, they're taken back home to St. Petersburg (Hannibal), and back to a momentary tomfoolery. Tom's schemes don't free Jim. Only the death of Jim's owner, Mrs. Watson, sets him free. Only Huck's distaste for civilization ("Go West, Young Man!") frees him from the shackles of the South: "But I reckon I got to light out for the Territory ahead of the rest, because Aunt Sally she's going to adopt me and sivilize me, and I can't stand it. I been there before. the end. yours truly, huck finn."

Today the South is going through a moral assault on the old "sivilization" of systemic racism, where freeing a slave from his "rightful" owner means going to hell. And the South is of course not the only region of this country with a strong sense of local habitation that has undergone transformation. New England has its own. In Concord, Massachusetts, history is prodding at Sleepy Hollow cemetery where writers once lay cozily near one another on Author's Ridge—Ralph Waldo Emerson, Henry David Thoreau, Nathaniel Hawthorne, Louisa May Alcott and her father, Bronson. New stories are being learned. Contemporary southerners may still be collecting together in that old-fashioned Concord way, still coming home. But home rumbles with thunderstorms of the past. And that lightning illuminates ghosts in their graves.

I live in Hillsborough, North Carolina. It's not very large, but you can swing a dead possum and smack a dozen southern writers in the face, many of us repatriated from the North. The truth is, it's not that we can't go home again; it's that we can't help it.

My mother, a southerner, a public schoolteacher, a lover of books and of those who wrote them, told me when I was still in elementary school, "You're southern, you're Irish. Be a writer or you'll end up in jail." In my teens I wrote sonnets in purple ink, slipping them in the tasseled boot of a majorette. In graduate school, far from the South, I wrote a novel, inspired in part by my mother's advice and by the mad recitations of an old English teacher from home who had floated through our cafeteria reciting Edgar Allan Poe to nobody in particular and whispering to us as she passed by, "I am looking for the next Thomas Wolfe. Is it you?" (Madness was no reason to fire her. She was a native of the town and from a good family. The South doesn't mind insanity as long as it's local.)

What it is to be a southerner always informs my fiction. Justin Savile wants to talk about his preference for the Old South over the New, even when I write him in London.

In the past a Hillston homicide came out of the Piedmont particularities of our town, its tobacco and textiles, its red clay farms and magnolia shaded university, its local people tied to land or town or college or family, it came out of something distinctive and therefore traceable. But that world is as distant as my grandparents' straw hats and pony carts, and in the Hillston we live in today, there are no landmarks to guide us.

Later in the day, Justin heads to meet his friend Cuddy Mangum, who is decked out in the biggest office in Hillston with a pair of cozy loafers that symbolizes his new promotion to chief. When Justin comes into the office ready to argue, he seizes on the tub of Kentucky Fried Chicken Cuddy is enjoying.

"Hail the new millennium. Everybody in America can eat the same trash now," I grumbled.

Cuddy gave me an ironic snort. "I never knew a man so incensed by junk food." He spun his hands in a tumbling circle. "I say roll out the polyester carpet for the new millennium. Let it roll, let it rock 'n roll, right on over the past. The *Old* South's got a lot worse to answer for than Colonel Sanders' family-pack."

The second Hillston novel, *Time's Witness*, the novel Cuddy narrates, has as the underpinning of its murder mystery how white supremacist militias are manipulated to serve corporate and political agendas and how the disproportionate use of capital punishment functions as a racist tool.

Whenever I'm asked why I, a "literary novelist," turn to the mystery, I rather grumpily reject the generic distinction. Long ago Knopf pressed me not to publish *Uncivil Seasons* after having written a novel like *Dingley Falls* and, youthfully arrogant at the time, I asked if they would shelve *The Sound and the Fury* in the literature section but put *Intruder in the Dust* among the "lower" mysteries?

A murder mystery (all of Dickens's novels could be so described) can be a way to enlarge the canvas beyond the relational and domestic, beyond the intimate confines of much modern fiction. It brings in police and courts and prisons, juries and judges, different occupations, different classes. It moves your story into a public realm where plots have moral and political and social dimensions, where private acts have consequences beyond the personal.

All stories, like all lives, are mystery stories. Everyone listens to stories to meet strangers and learn their plots. We are all detectives searching for clues to our connections. The heart of fiction is always to get at the secrets. That there should be such a strong southern heritage to the mystery therefore makes perfect sense. To solve murders, detectives must unearth all the buried social and familial entanglements that led to the crimes. Here in the South, the roots of our lives are tangled together, deep in a shared rich and often painful past.

That South has changed enormously over the decades that I've been writing about it. In my youth, almost all the people in North Carolina were natives of the state, and the joke was that our license plate mottos should read, "Five Million People; Fifteen Last Names." The population is now much more heterogeneous, and now the jokes are of this variety: that CARY stands for "Containment Area for Retired Yankees." But we should note that many of the jokes reveal how the South continues to define itself mythically, as a place that can be defined. Haunted by our virtues and our sins, we create and sustain ourselves out of those fictions. That's why so many of us are writers, and why all of us are storytellers.

On one of my writer's pilgrimages through America, I went to Asheville, North Carolina, to see Thomas Wolfe's grave. Next to his grave is that of his brother. On the gravestone the inscription reads, "Luke of Look Homeward Angel." It's not true that you can't go home again. You can't help it.

My novels evolve from the characters who inhabit them. The minute I hear the voice of a narrator, from word one of page one, I am listening to that character's voice. Narrators are characters too. The narrator of *Handling Sin* is very different from that of *The Last Noel* (a Christmas tale set here in a fictional version of my Hillsborough home). But all the storytellers of my fiction, and all those who live their lives inside the covers of my books are, I trust, equally at home in their birthplaces. Now they live in North Carolina, in the red clay landscape of my imagination. Here's the first paragraph of the first book I wrote after I came home again, the opening of *Four Corners of the Sky*.

In small towns between the North Carolina Piedmont and the coast the best scenery is often in the sky. On flat sweeps of red clay and scrub pine the days move monotonously, safely, but above, in the blink of an eye, dangerous clouds can boil out of all four corners of the sky and do away with the sun so fast that, in the sudden quiet, birds fly shrieking to shelter. The flat slow land starts to shiver and anything can happen.

NOTES

1. Jack Kerouac, in a June 29, 1962, *Life* magazine tribute to former Horace Mann classmate Eddie Gilbert ("He Went on the Road, as Jack Kerouac Says," p. 22).
2. Alison Beard, "Life's Work: An Interview with Isabel Allende," *Harvard Business Review*, May 2016, https://hbr.org/2016/05/isabel-allende.
3. James Joyce to Arthur Power in a discussion of *Ulysses*, *Irish Free Times*, October 1922.
4. Flannery O'Connor, from "The Fiction Writer and His Country," from *The Living Novel: A Symposium* (New York: Macmillan, 1957), 157–164.

MARIA TERESA UNGER PALMER

¿*Mi Tierra?* (Home)land for North Carolina Latinos

I CAME TO THE United States from Guatemala in 1978, with every intention of returning home after college, either to my dad's next international posting or to Perú, the land of my birth. As happens to the best of us, I fell in love, married, and stayed. Nine years later, while attending seminary and contemplating the future I would help build for my first child, I became a US citizen. Mike and I, both educators, built a very traditional family, first in Kentucky and then in Virginia.

Accustomed to being the only resident "foreigner" in our small college town in Virginia, I was surprised by the number of brown-skinned people I saw when we moved to Chapel Hill, North Carolina in 1994. During college and seminary, I had ministered to migrant farmworkers in Arizona and in the tomato and cucumber fields and apple orchards of Virginia, so I knew about migrant farm laborers. But what were these young men and even whole families doing in Chapel Hill? I asked fellow students. They had no idea. Neither did my professors. I asked one of my advisors if working with the new immigrants might not be a good area of study. "They are not on my radar screen," she said. Boy, did she miss a wonderful opportunity! Today, most of the enrollment growth in our public schools comes from immigrant families and, with little research to guide us, we are struggling to meet their needs.

In the 1990s two forces were most responsible for the increase in immigration to the state: the economic boom in North Carolina that created a huge need for blue-collar skilled and unskilled labor and NAFTA (North American Free Trade Agreement). As cheap American corn flooded Mexican markets, many young men in Mexican communities found it impossible to scrape a living from their land. The dozens of young men arriving daily in the Triad and the Triangle—Greensboro, Raleigh, Siler City, and even Chapel Hill—were here because, in desperation, they had decided to look for work in *el Norte*, and North Carolina is where their *coyotes* had told them they could find jobs.

Shortly after my arrival, I started volunteering at the IFC (Interfaith Council of Social Services) as a translator. I made phone calls to waiting cousins and friends of friends. I translated for employers who dropped by to hire workers on the spot. I saw the look of incredulity and joy when a young man was offered $6 an hour and guaranteed sixty hours a week by a landscaper, who also wanted to hire me to help him get all his new Mexican workers "legal papers." It was a time when explaining that "there is no mechanism for getting these workers visas" was met with a shrug. "No problem. We'll work something out."

In the next few years, it would become commonplace to hear Spanish around town and see Hispanic food sections at Walmart and Food Lion stores and to see immigrant crews cleaning office buildings, staffing fast-food restaurants, landscaping our parks, and holding the caution flags around road construction.

I remember that fall running into a young man who had been dropped off in downtown Chapel Hill and found his way to the IFC offices on Wilson Street, next to the church I was attending and where I would later establish a Spanish-language congregation, *Iglesia Unida de Cristo de Chapel Hill*. He had not eaten since the van stopped in Texas the day before. He had a blank Social Security card and was ready to go to work, he said; he only needed help finding out where to get the Social Security number to write on the card. He had come from a small communal farm in Mexico—an *éjido*— an hour from the nearest small town in the state of San Luis. From shared lands and dirt floors and mud walls and animals that roam the dirt streets, and one central phone booth for the whole village to Tar Heel basketball traffic and thousands of people on Franklin Street. From eggs from your backyard hens and homemade tortillas and beans to shelves of frozen and canned food and restaurants where a single meal costs more than a week's wages back home.

In smaller numbers than the Mexicans and Central Americans who came in the late nineties, the Colombians followed. While they did not have harrowing tales of walking across the border or hiding in suffocating trucks, many Colombians had their own traumatic experiences, uncovered gradually, painfully, as they settled in and began dealing with the nightmares and traumas born of kidnappings, extortion, and murders by guerrillas or drug traffickers. Among the Colombians who found their way to Iglesia, many were women and some were young widows. I remember an intact young family with two boys that visited our church in 2000 or 2001. They must have been spared by the war, I thought. I was wrong. The father stood by the open door throughout the service. "Maybe a reluctant Catholic, wary of a woman preacher?" I wondered, as I observed him nervously scanning the congregation and the parking lot. He was Catholic, but curious and open-minded about women ministers. What concerned him, I found out later, was the open door, and the access it provided to possible armed intruders. He asked if I would consider locking the doors to keep the families safe. A former surveyor who had loved exploring uncharted territories, he had been kidnapped by the guerrillas and then rescued in a government raid where two other hostages, his coworkers, were killed. To feel safe he needed to be inside, behind locked doors.

I recently visited his family, now living in a neighboring county. Fourteen years later, he is a US citizen and the father of three handsome boys, two naturalized and one native-born. This is now home, he tells me, but only because of the deep friendships he's made and because of his children. They consider themselves "Tar Heels," he jokes. The oldest is applying to the University of North Carolina and is sure to get in. He owns his home now, and a family business, and his connection with the land is through his sons. And while he still works inside, he does enjoy playing outside with the kids in his fenced-in backyard.

Another Colombian who came to Iglesia was the traumatized mother of eleven grown children, grandmother of "about forty," and great-grandmother of four. She had been a landowner in the *llanos* (the cattle area between the jungle and the mountains) and by all accounts was a true force of nature. All her children had been born at home because she climbed out the window of the hospital and returned to her home by boat after her husband left her in the city to give birth to their firstborn. "If all the natives can have their children and go back to work the next day," she told me, "I figured I could too." She had learned many cures from the Indian women as well as many ways to facilitate labor.

When I met this amazing woman, she could not sleep and found herself crying for no reason. She had flashbacks where she saw the mutilated bodies of the sixteen farmworkers the guerrillas killed when they invaded her land. She would relive the weeks she hid in the jungle, tending to those in the group suffering from dengue fever or malaria. It took weeks of prayer and what she called her "gardening therapy" for the healing to begin. She would get up at 5:30 in the morning and weed the yard. She planted everything she could buy or "borrow" from friends that she deemed useful: herbs and "infusions" (lemongrass, mint), tomatoes, peppers, potatoes, and even fruit trees.

She lives in a rented room in somebody else's home; her family and even her landlord chide her for spending so much time and money planting trees and vegetables and tending somebody else's garden. "The land belongs to everyone," she says, "and it is our job to improve it. Somebody else planted the fruit trees that feed us today." About four years after her arrival in Orange County, North Carolina, Mrs. E became a Health Promoter with our health department and is now also a respected doula among the Hispanic immigrant community.

In 1995 I started a small Bible study to create a little oasis of understanding and hope for the newcomers. By 1996, it had become a new church, known around town as

Iglesia Unida, and a 24/7 immigrant clearinghouse and helpline. We started a bilingual preschool and support groups; we furnished apartments and did healing services, memorials for relatives being buried far away. We provided a surrogate family to the grieving grandson who couldn't attend the funeral of the woman who had raised him; we called dishonest bosses and demanded payment for desperately needed wages. We mediated in sometimes amusing, sometimes heartbreaking misunderstandings. We kept prayer vigils when wives and children were known to be making their way across dangerous borders. We celebrated when the first Iglesia Unida family bought its own home. We blessed the opening of the first business. We organized every kind of ceremony, from home dedications, to hybrid Christmas *Posadas/Novenas*, to First Communions (never seen in a Protestant church in North Carolina, I am sure), to our own community "biblical" Halloween festival (some of my congregants were convinced their children would be poisoned if allowed to trick-or-treat).

A UNC anthropology student who visited my church for a semester project called it "an experiment in creating an immigrant theology." If I was experimenting in doing immigrant theology, my flock was experimenting in becoming North Carolinians.

As an immigrant, I realize that if I ever feel like I don't belong, it has less to do with the land or the people of North Carolina than with the difficulty of trying to grow new roots in new soil. It is easy for a little seedling, but painful and nigh near impossible for a grown tree. I am lucky I was somewhere in between a seedling and a grown-up. At times, "transplanted trees" feel as if a strong wind would easily topple us, the roots are so weak and shallow. We might look strong and even provide shade for our families, but it takes so much work to stay upright!

For some, the roots that connect us to the language of our community are missing. Our mother tongue is part of the soil that nurtures us. To be healthy and create human connections, we have to be able to tell others how we feel. Without language skills there is little learning, little growth, and little understanding. I have seen parents suffer when their children learn English and they cannot understand what they are saying ("because it sometimes sounds like gibberish") but also because they feel useless, unable to parent.

The roots that connect us with family and neighbors are hard to grow back and require reciprocity. The deep web of relationships that can be tapped for support is missing for many immigrants. "Well, I am lonely and bored," a young dishwasher says when I tell him I am writing an article about immigrants and wondering how recently relocated Mexican country folks are doing in the Town of Chapel Hill in 2015. When you don't know people, he explains, you only have home and work, work and home. "*Extraño los jardines*" (I miss the gardens), he adds. "You know, public parks where you can go with your family or friends, where there are clowns and vendors, and rides for the kids, and flowers and benches." A sad smile and a distant look tell me he is remembering those good times. "*No hay ningún lugar como su tierra*" (There is no place like your own land, your homeland).

I asked my mother to give me her definition of *su tierra*, which literally means "your land." "It is your small city or community, but it is not a geographically defined place," she explains. "It is more what you feel, the place you feel you belong to." However, she has to add this caveat: it depends on where you are and who asks. When we lived in Guatemala, she reminds me, *nuestra tierra* was Perú. But if another Peruvian were to ask, we'd have to say Lima, or even just our district, Miraflores.

As a pastor, as an educator, and as a mother, I have sought to give immigrants a community where they could grow new roots: a community where they can establish new traditions, a network of homes where they feel welcomed and expected, where their language is understood, and perhaps most important, where they can contribute their wisdom and love. Inviting immigrant parents to teach a class, do a demonstration, create a bulletin board, serve on a committee is all part of growing new roots.

Of course, growing new roots requires a willingness to see the new community as a permanent, or at least long-term, place. For some immigrants, this feels like forsaking their ties to their families and their homeland. I will never forget the reaction of a young woman when we read the parable of the prodigal son in a home Bible study. Following the reading, she burst into tears. "That's me!" she cried. "I left my father and my mother. I used money that they could have used to fix up their house to pay for the visa and the airfare. I came to build my own future, and now as they get old and need me more, I will be far away, struggling." It was the heart-wrenching realization that every immigrant comes to when the excitement of the new adventure wears off: the enormous cost of separation, of leaving behind our homeland.

There are too many sad songs about immigration. Mexican corridos, Cuban ballads, Argentinian tangos, Peruvian valses, and even church praise songs. But immigrants, while longing for the tastes and smells and sounds—and even the soil itself—of our homelands, are a future-looking bunch. While we cry for aging parents and intimate friends, we are also learning and writing new songs, planting gardens, inventing a hybrid culture, and growing new roots. It is possible to thrive in new soil. It may even be possible, I think, to one day be able to honestly call two places *mi tierra*.

NOTE

All quotations are from oral interviews conducted by the author. The 2015 UNC's Kenan-Flagler Business School report on "Demographic and Economic Impacts of International Migration to North Carolina" contains thirty-four pages of detailed facts about the people who are making North Carolina part of the Global South. Among the fascinating facts included in that report are the following: (1.) Today, there are roughly 750,000 foreign-born residents living in North Carolina, up from twenty-two thousand in 1960, an increase of 3,303.7 percent. (2.) Foreign-born residents account for an estimated 7.7 percent of North Carolina's population. (3.) Our immigrant newcomers are more likely to be people of color—Mexican (37%), Salvadorian, Honduran, Guatemalan, Indian, Chinese, Vietnamese, Korean, and Filipino—than to be non-Hispanic white.

AMANDA BELLOWS

"As Natural as Rain or Madness"

A Conversation with Richard Grant

ICHARD GRANT, a British writer who has traveled around the world and recently made Mississippi his home, is a quintessentially global southerner. Grant's interests are as wide-ranging as his journeys; he has spent time working on books, articles, and other projects in Mexico, Tanzania, Italy, and the American West. Drawn to the state of Mississippi, he recently decided to purchase a home there.

South Writ Large communicated with Mr. Grant about his new book, *Dispatches from Pluto: Lost and Found in the Mississippi Delta* (2015), a lively account of his first year living in the Delta.

Dispatches from Pluto: Lost and Found in the Mississippi Delta **tells the story of your decision to relocate from New York City to Pluto, Mississippi, where you and your family make a new life for yourselves. What feature of the Mississippi Delta most attracted you?**

We knew nothing about the Delta when we decided to buy a remote farmhouse there, thirty miles from the nearest supermarket. It was the setting that attracted me: big sky, golden light, cotton fields and cypress swamps, birds everywhere, deer in the woods.

What aspects of daily life in Mississippi most surprised you?

Shooting squirrels with pink rifles to promote breast cancer awareness. Photographs in the newspapers of five-year-old girls holding up the antlers of deer they had just shot. The extreme racial segregation in Delta schools, with the whites in private academies and Blacks in failing public schools. The ability of people to hold enormous family trees in their heads and remember the maiden names of each other's great-grandmothers. The custom of giving guests a sixteen-ounce Styrofoam cup full of ice and liquor for the drive home.

How does the South and Mississippi in particular live up to its reputation for hospitality and friendliness? What were the ways you felt welcomed and what ways did you feel yourself to be an outsider?

The hospitality has been incredible, wonderful, staggering. On our second day in the house, the nearest neighbors came over with wine and a selection of firearms to shoot. Noting our lack of furniture, they came back two days later with beds, couches, a kitchen table and chairs, armchairs, all on permanent loan for as long as we wanted it. Noting that we had only one vehicle, they gave us the keys to one of their cars. Later on, they adopted us into their family and hosted our wedding. I always feel like an outsider, but a very welcome outsider.

With whom did you become friends?

As I said, the neighboring Thompsons became more like family than friends. Probably my closest friend was William "Monk" Neal, a Black man whose family used to work for the white Thompson family. We spent a lot of time grilling meat, drinking whiskey, listening to music, and talking about the complexities and contradictions of Mississippi race relations. I also became friends with Bill Luckett, the mayor of Clarksdale, and Morgan Freeman, the actor, who lives in the Delta. And the blues singer T-Model Ford (RIP). And Sam Olden, a one-hundred-and-two-year-old former CIA agent with an amazing art collection and dazzling intellect. And the dentist who operated on death row prisoners at Parchman prison. Many others. No shortage of characters in the Delta, and I found it a very easy place to make friends.

What pastimes did you find interesting relative to the different institutions and activities that make up Mississippi's culture, i.e., church, academy, sports, arts, music, etc.?

I found the Black churches a great deal more enjoyable than the white churches. Mississippi's obsession with college football didn't rub off on me, although I did enjoy tailgating at Ole Miss. Hunting is the great pastime in the Delta, and that did rub off on me. I had never done any hunting before moving to Mississippi, and within a year, there were deer, duck, doves, rabbits, bullfrogs, wild hog, and alligator meat in my freezer.

I was wonderfully spoiled for live music. One of my Pluto neighbors is a gospel musician, and he would come over with his group and play at our parties. The phenomenal Rev. John Wilkins performed with his gospel-blues band down the road at Pluto. I got to know a blues singer called Jimmy "Duck" Holmes who owns a juke joint in Bentonia, MS. There is so much musical talent in Mississippi. Even karaoke night in a small-town bar can be amazing.

As a British man living in a rural region within the United States, did you ever feel out of place in your new home?

I always felt out of place, but in a good way. I felt very free and alive, and open to new possibilities.

When you tell your fellow countrymen about the South, how do you express the concept of the South that differentiates it from elsewhere?

What differentiates the South as a region, more than anything, is its shared history: slavery, secession, losing a war, Reconstruction, the rebuilding of white supremacy through Jim Crow laws and KKK terrorism, battling again over race during the civil rights movement. The past is more present in the South than the rest of America. The hold of church and family is stronger. It's also a place of extraordinary human warmth and kindness, and contradictions here are as natural as rain or madness.

One of the most interesting chapters of your book is "Grabbing Smoke," a discussion of racism in Mississippi. In it, you argue that when one attempts to "measure and quantify prejudice itself that it all turn[s] to smoke." What assumptions did you have about racism in the South prior to your arrival in Pluto? Has your understanding of race relations changed at all since you moved to Mississippi?

The hardest thing to understand is that love and closeness also exist between the races in Mississippi, right alongside hate, prejudice, distrust, and a deep impulse to self-segregate. Race relations are layered and complex here and defy easy explanation. You often hear, "In the South, we love the individual and hate the race." That to me, requires a considerable feat of mental gymnastics, or a psychiatric evaluation, but it's a normal everyday thing here, and most people don't question it.

From your experience, is it possible to see Mississippi as a laboratory for the increasing necessity for people around the world to learn to live with others of racial, ethnic, and cultural diversity?

Yes. When circumstances push them together, Black and white get along with each other extraordinarily well here. But most of the time they choose not to. There is so much distrust on both sides, but slowly, gradually, it's breaking down, one relationship at a time. People here are uncommonly stubborn and suspicious of change, which is part of the problem. I would hope that in other places it happens quicker.

There has been a long-standing pattern of Mississippi writers—Eudora Welty, Elizabeth Spencer, Willie Morris, Bill Ferris—who moved northward or even abroad to find literary inspiration. How does your experience of moving to Mississippi compare with theirs?

It doesn't. Mississippi writers are so entangled with their roots. I'm not really from anywhere. I was born in Malaysia, lived in Kuwait as a boy, then London. I've lived in twenty different houses on four different continents. I'm rootless and have no strong conception of home, which is almost unimaginable for these Mississippi writers.

As a global traveler, have you identified any elements of southern culture that remind you of behaviors, traditions, or social rituals in other countries where you've spent time?

Mississippi sometimes reminds me of Ireland. The hold of the church and the extended family. The pleasure in strong drink, storytelling, and mischief. The appreciation for talent.

What will your next project be?

I'm not sure. I've been reading a lot of Mississippi history books lately, and something might come out of that. I've also been consulting on a new documentary about ending infanticide in southern Ethiopia. It's called *Omo Child: The River and the Bush*. And there's talk in Los Angeles of turning *Dispatches from Pluto* into a television series.

CHERYL ISAAC

The Forgotten Town,
The Forgotten Backwater

"DON'T GO THERE; you wouldn't fit in," my city friends told me, slightly amused by the prospect of my moving to this side of the Appalachian Mountains, their eyebrows raised with intrigue and bafflement. "They call it the town that time forgot," a realtor informed my husband and me as we toured Grundy, Virginia. Well water still flowed through the faucets of some homes, staining dishwashers and bathtubs, and mold (and in some cases water) still lingered in basements that hadn't been lifted after the town's most recent flood.

Yet this forgotten town was intriguing because it reminded me of Liberia, the "forgotten African backwater," as Polish journalist Ryszard Kapuściński called the country where I was born and raised—the country I was having difficulty writing about.[1] I didn't know how to express it, but as I laid in my room at the only hotel in the town, I sensed that Grundy would be the place to help me forget; forget who I was in that hotel, so that I could write about who I was in my native country. I just knew that the town's generous mountains, flowing creeks, warm skies, light mist, and spunky birds would help me complete the first draft of my book about a formerly peaceful Liberian childhood assaulted by war and trauma.

Upon entering Grundy, you know that you're in the belly of southwest Virginia, with mountain roads uniquely steep in some places and obtrusively curvy in others. You don't need an almanac to tell you that once you drive along routes like 460 or 624, you won't experience anything else as thrilling and terrifying, with v-shaped terrains that take you to Bristol, Tennessee, or Bluefield, Virginia, if you continue to Route 19. Grundy is coal country that stands proud and tall, where fumes and gray sheets of dirt from passing coal trucks rise with the sun in the morning. It is a town of the strong, the brave, the miners—where you're at first taken aback by the "black lung" signs posted by lawyers, doctors, and insurance companies; where the first time you walk into the post office, the postal worker at the counter says "ya reckon" in the middle of a conversation with a customer, and you're completely dumbfounded with excitement because this is the first time the phrase has jumped out of one of your books and skipped around your eardrums.

We came here at a good time, they tell us, because Grundy has grown up. It has been over a decade since the law school where my husband teaches was introduced to the town. There is now a brand-new Walmart, a shopping plaza, and a choice between Mexican, Chinese, or American cuisine. Daily construction along Route 460 has been initiated to improve the infrastructure and accommodate new buildings and a potential housing development. The town that is said to dislike outsiders has graciously accommodated lots of us: some young, some old, some graduate students, some professionals, each of us nestled closely into the mountainside.

To most people, our decision about where my husband should accept a law school faculty position was obvious: say yes to one of the schools in one of the "normal" cities. Yet even after we had driven through town for the first time, on a dark, snowy evening, staring wide-eyed at the houses snuggled comfortably in the valley below, perturbed by the crookedness of the roads and intimidated by the bravado of the truckers, we chose Grundy.

How could I tell them that once in Grundy, I felt God in its mountains and creeks, looming beside me on mountain trails, flowing from springs, swinging from tree branches and church steeples? How could I explain the same soothing presence that kept me sane when I sought shelter at a church compound for two years during the 1990 Liberian Civil War?

Nestled between the former French and British colonies, Ivory Coast and Sierra Leone, respectively, Liberia is the first African republic and the only American-influenced West African country. A country that has suffered no major natural disaster, it is known for its flatlands, lagoons and oceans. Founded in 1847 with the help of the American Colonization Society, Liberia is where American freed slaves built a home for themselves. They brought with them bits and pieces of the only world they knew—America—causing a divide between themselves and the indigenous Liberians. However, once we found ourselves huddled together at our church shelter during the war, seeking cover on the floors and beneath beds and benches, this divide seemed miniscule.

Now Liberia, once the heartthrob of West Africa nicknamed "Small America," is Africa's prodigal daughter and America's forgotten sister. Liberian natives who have left, scarred by war, often ask each other, "Why would you want to go back *there*?"

The same thing happens in Grundy.

"You go to school here, sweetie?" a Grundy native and Walmart store clerk asked me.

"No, ma'am."

"Work here?"

"No, ma'am," I answered again with a slight smile, because I knew what was coming next.

She stopped bagging my groceries, gave a quick glance over her shoulders, and faced me with the concerned eyes a grandmother reserves for her sick grandbabies. Her eyebrows were pulled together in silent thought when she placed her hands on my arm and whispered, "*Why* are you *here?*"

Some mornings, when I feel Grundy beneath my feet as I walk my dog or exercise, I'm reminded of Annie Dillard's words, "They say of nature that it conceals with a grand nonchalance, and they say of vision that it is a deliberate gift,"[2] because in order to truly see Grundy, you must have the kind of vision that surpasses its narrow roads and limited shopping; in order to see the gift that its nature conceals, a gift so rare that once the veil is lifted from your eyes, you see the town for what it really is: a treasure valley. Hidden compartments that conceal the most obscure revelations, valleys that dazzle with the kind of sensations that force you to slow down for a minute to, say, write a book.

When I write about something as personal as childhood and family, of something as traumatic as the loss of childhood and family, the mountains of Grundy become as necessary as the shell of a turtle, its shelter as private as the inner compartments of my mind. There are no rules in Grundy's mountains, no codes to entrap you. You can't even count on your iPhone weather app to be close to accurate like you would in other cities because like Danny Glover's character said in the movie *Switchback*, "Weather don't make the rules, mountains do." Mountain life is an existential burrow that propels you forward, deeper and deeper into its folds, until from beneath its shadows, while you await the sun's slow dance around its peaks, while you gaze in awe at its sharp, rugged beauty and encompassing breadth, you become deeply aware of who you are, who you are not, and who you can become, because nothing explains the baffling world better than its indescribable nature.

From Liberia to New York City to Columbus, Ohio and now Grundy—I am not alone in my path here. Grundy is as global as its inhabitants: the law students from Africa and Asia; the mission school that boards international students just across the street from where I live; the bird that wakes me up on hot spring mornings with its part-whistling, part-humming, the same one that woke me up on mornings during the rainy season in Liberia (one day I will learn your name, dear one).

Sitting next to Slate Creek with my eyes closed, sniffing for words, sounds, thoughts, and feelings, I am aware that, just like Liberia, Grundy will live on, despite its refusal to conform, its dare to be different. *If Grundy can survive its deviance, if Liberia can survive its incongruity, so can I.* In moments like these, I am fully aware of how this southern town has transformed me, and unexplainable joy crawls from my belly, sweeps across my face, and becomes one with the creek, slowly treading its way through Edgewater Drive, through Grundy, through Buchanan County, through Virginia, and onwards, ready and willing to connect with a destiny that is bigger, more expansive, and even more challenging.

NOTES

1. Ryszard Kapuściński, *The Shadow of the Sun* (New York: Vintage, 2001).
2. Annie Dillard, *Pilgrim at Tinker Creek* (New York: McGraw-Hill, 2000), 18.

Bo Bartlett, *Open Gate*, 2011, courtesy of the artist

VISUAL CULTURES

JILL McCORKLE

At the Intersection of Emotions

Jill McCorkle on the Art of Bo Bartlett

OSTALGIA IS A WORD people often shy away from, seeing it as a sentimental, romanticized representation of what was, instead of relying on the original definition of pain and ache—a wave of time- or homesickness for what is past. That kind of longing—the blend of comfort and joy with sadness and loss—is what I am most drawn to as a writer and reader, and I am constantly trying to seek balance between the two. I am drawn to literature and music and art and everyday moments that make me aware of such an intersection of emotion. The art of Bo Bartlett places me in that very satisfying intersection.

My first experience with Bartlett's wonderful art was when his painting *Young Life* was used to illustrate a piece I wrote for the *Oxford American*. I was struck by the sharp, beautiful clarity as well as the direct gaze all three subjects projected; they are all looking, and yet, it seems each is in a very different place emotionally. At first glance it seems the equivalent of a simple coming-of-age story, the attention to the physical details of the setting striking and memorable—the truck and deer on top of it, the brilliant blue sky. The young boy stands removed from the couple I assume to be his parents, his stick pointing in the opposite direction of his father's gun. If I were to write the short story to accompany it, I would be drawn to the three different points of view of the moment. The awareness of three separate experiences within one frozen moment creates a quiet but powerful tension.

Bartlett often captures a moment in time that is easily nostalgic—a homecoming bonfire or Christmas pageant—and yet what is consistent in his work is the presence of the Other; he encapsulates the comfort of tradition but also infuses it with a wisdom or dark knowledge of what is to come. I have not studied art. I only know what catches my eye and pulls me in so that there is no looking away. I am drawn to sharp contrasts of light and dark, both literally and figuratively. I am drawn to suggested narrative, and Bartlett's work is filled with narratives.

In *Homecoming* there seems to be a novel's worth of storytelling—the referee in conversation off to the side, the group of people in the distance, the red convertible awaiting the exit. The fire is just large enough to suggest that things might leap out of control, and the varying emotional expressions of the three couples suggest the grown-up years ahead of them.

It is not lost on me that Bo Bartlett shares the hometown of one of my favorite writers. Carson McCullers also was born in Columbus, Georgia, and she too could create those pangs of time or homesickness with her writing while also conveying the wisdom and knowledge of a much broader story. You only need to read *The Heart Is a Lonely Hunter* to witness this. That novel, like many of Bartlett's paintings, captures individual narratives that each, like separate instruments, blend together to create the symphony of the whole. McCullers managed to give every character a voice, and I feel the same is true of Bartlett's subjects. McCullers hit chords of the grotesque and fantastic while remaining firmly rooted in a recognizable setting. Bartlett accomplishes this same feat in his painting *Leviathan*, a retelling of the biblical Jonah story within a wholly contemporary setting.

One of my favorite recent paintings by Bartlett is *Open Gate*. I was immediately drawn to the tricycle and how, as with Eggleston's famous photograph,[1] the object itself conveys the child's point of view. In Bartlett's painting, the young boy's head is turned, looking out the gate, which serves as the other focal point. There is such power between the two points—where the boy is in the present moment and where he might be within seconds. The painting is filled with anticipation and is perfectly perched in that precarious place between what is known and what is unknown. I felt torn at first glance between a child's will and a parent's control. The gate is open. Something will happen. I can't see the expression on his face, only the direction of that wheel. I saw this beautiful image and could not get it out of my mind. The painting pulls us in and makes us remember what it felt like to be a child and see that open gate while at the same time lending the parental perspective of witnessing your child *seeing* the open gate. There is exhilaration. There is fear. There is a time-sickness for when you yourself first glimpsed the gate and also for the time before your children first glimpsed it. The seemingly simple composition, like that of *Young Life*, is anything but. *Open Gate* filled me with so many conflicting emotions. It was only later upon reading about the image that I learned Bartlett had lost a child, and yet, the narrative still is one that provides balance between that homesick feeling for a particular joy or comfort and the solemn knowledge of what the future might hold.

Bartlett's work is inspiring, prompting viewers to reach back into their own trunk of memories to find those that have a similar power. In *The Ballad of the Sad Cafe*, McCullers wrote beautifully about the imbalance between the lover and the beloved. "First of all, love is a joint experience between two persons—but the fact that it is a joint experience does not mean that it is a similar experience to the two people involved. There are the lover and the beloved, but these two come from different countries."[2]

I think that Bo Bartlett finds that imbalance, that complicated narrative of life. The person with eyes closed in meditation or looking directly at the viewer. The gaze that sees something beyond the frame of the painting. There is always the broader perspective, which for me is what makes his work so incredibly moving. I know but I don't know. I'm there as participant but also as witness. This person is in the moment, but this other one is staring me in the eye with a kind of foreboding knowledge of what lies ahead. There are so many dimensions emotionally. Layers upon layers. I long for what is familiar even despite the haunting sense of foreboding.

I have mentioned *The Heart Is a Lonely Hunter*, a work that realistically creates and brings to life a southern town of a particular time. Within this familiar setting, we find characters who represent every walk of life, especially those who, for whatever reason—race or religion, physical disability or heartbreak—are removed from the path of the mainstream. Likewise, Bo Bartlett takes on the great challenging expanse of human emotion within the most routine settings. There is often a background of everyday ordinariness. But look closer. The scene is never simple, and I am always left imagining *what next*? Likewise, we anticipate the next work from this extraordinary artist.

NOTES

1. William Eggleston, *Tricycle (Memphis)*, ca. 1975.
2. Carson McCullers, *The Ballad of the Sad Cafe* (New York: Bantam, 1967), 26.

JEFFERSON CURRIE II

Putting Scrap in a Pasture

Vollis Simpson's Whirligigs

**HEN I WOULD SIT** and talk with Vollis Simpson at his repair shop, near Lucama, Wilson County, North Carolina, he would often voice his irritation about folks who littered and wasted. He railed against those who discarded bags of garbage, mattresses, tires, and other detritus in the woods and fields on his land, telling me about times he tracked down the culprits through what they left behind, went to their houses, and demanded they clean up the trash. One afternoon, when he was having trouble getting around, he had me stake a sign into the dirt and gravel Vollis Shop Road, just behind a mattress and box spring one of those rogues had thrown out the night before. The poster board sign lettered with marker read, "Sorry S.O.B. $200 Reward." Sometimes Vollis would tell me about how farming had changed, how the land was ruined nowadays by farmers who insisted on plowing when it was too wet, making a mess of the fields. In the late summer and early fall he would tell me to go and glean the sweet potatoes that were left behind by farmers who rented his fields for their crops. Even when he had gone to his cane, Vollis would drive out into those fields and throw dozens of misshapen potatoes into the back of his pickup truck so he could give them away at his shop when folks came by to look at his whirligigs; every day he would put food scraps out on a covered picnic table he had designed and built so the animals—squirrels, raccoons, birds—would have something to eat throughout the day. Vollis would often voice strong opinions about most issues, and even though people knew that his whirligigs were created from scrapped objects, I was intrigued that many folks didn't link his propensity to collect metal for sculptures with ideas like conservation and recycling.

From 1951 to the early 1980s, Vollis Simpson's repair shop was neat, clean, and in pretty tidy shape, but over the past thirty years, the area around the shop became a collection of parts and objects he purchased from manufacturing plants, salvage yards, and a host of other businesses in and around Wilson County. It was open

Vollis Simpson, *Time Machine*, photo by Jefferson Currie II

storage, an inventory that Vollis would draw from when he was building his kinetic sculptures that stretch out and up to gigantic proportions. If it could catch air, enable spinning, gleam, shine, twirl, or whirl, Vollis would check it out to see if he could use it to build a whirligig or windmill. Before he began building and erecting his sculptures along Wiggins Mill Road, he built a windmill while he was in the Army Air Corps in World War II. It was made to wash clothes on Saipan in the South Pacific. That war-built washing machine has often been cited in articles and stories about Vollis, but at times he ignored inquiries about the suds maker; instead, he would glow when he talked about the motorcycle he built as the war drew to a close. Even in his twenties, Vollis was creatively reusing scrapped and discarded items to build machines.

After the war ended and Vollis was back in Wilson County, he worked the farm he grew up on for a few years until he built a repair shop in 1951 on a sliver of land at a rural five-points intersection near his house. He based his business in the shop for over thirty years, repairing equipment and machines, building tow trucks and cranes out of army surplus vehicles, spraying tobacco fields with a self-propelled sprayer he invented, doing rigging work, towing, salvaging, and moving buildings like his father did when Vollis was growing up. He had a shop, but often he had work that kept him laboring all over the county and region. I have heard many times from people around the area that if someone needed something done—towing, moving a house or barn, moving machinery into a manufacturing plant—and no one else could do it, Vollis Simpson could do it. He honed his natural abilities in mechanics and engineering over many years of hard work until he became a master craftsman.

While he worked, he continued to repurpose materials to create distinct machines for various tasks. When the heating oil shortages and corresponding spike in prices crippled the country in the early 1970s, Vollis built a windmill that forced wood-heated air through the ductwork of his house. Although there was a little issue with smoke leakage, his talent in reclaiming objects for new and kinetic uses saved him money and the frustrations of coping through shortages that dragged on through the rest of the 1970s. Vollis was a maker, a builder, a creator, an inventor, and his supplies were often whatever he had held onto that he bought from junkyards, salvage yards, and various manufacturing plants.

In the late 1970s and early 1980s, Vollis decreased his workload a bit, transitioning to a shorter work week, and he decided to fill the time by building a few windmills and kinetic sculptures using the metal and other materials he had around the shop and his house. When asked why he started building windmills, Vollis said, "I had a lot of material left over and I didn't want to junk it or salvage it. I put most of it out there in the pasture." At first he worked part-time, mostly weekends and downtimes, but even working just a few days a month, after about ten years he built and erected around twenty separate pieces. For years people have referred to Vollis as an artist, which he would reference offhandedly at times, seemingly a bit amused by the word. Many took the word further, adding descriptors such as *folk*, *outsider*, or *visionary*, but those extra monikers seem problematic and pejorative, pushing him away from what really informed his work. Vollis had skills in mechanics, welding, engineering, and design, skills learned over a lifetime that were not that uncommon growing up farming and owning a repair shop in rural eastern North Carolina in the first half of the twentieth century. I think he was also born with more talents than most, which set him apart from others; he was special. But after spending time with him and talking with friends and family who knew him for years, I realized that Vollis also loved to work more than anyone I've ever known. The active process of making, building, constructing, crafting, painting—the work of creating one of his windmills—gave him pleasure. Combined, it's a powerful mix—that skill and talent and the pleasure he got from working as long and as hard as he could.

The first piece he put up, out in front of his shop near the corner of Vollis Shop Road and Wiggins Mill Road, is striking because it isn't a windmill or a whirligig.

A collection of old car parts, unusual curved steel bars, steel bicycle rims, a metal globe, an arrow cut from barn roofing tin, and what looks to be a perforated washing machine tub are assembled, painted red, white, green, yellow, and blue, covered with round vehicle reflectors and cut up road signs, mounted on a vehicle hub and erected on a pole. The kinetic sculpture resembles the satellite Sputnik, albeit a vibrantly painted version that moves and spins in the lightest of winds.

Although Vollis's first satellite-like piece was a strikingly abstract sculpture, many of his early works were figurative—men riding bicycles and unicycles; a man riding a cart whipping a mule whose legs move back and forth when the wind pushes a large steel farm wheel; two men sawing a log with a crosscut saw while their dog stands behind them, tail wagging. A few planes and helicopters, some small, are scattered about, made of wood or PVC pipe and attached to larger pieces; some planes are much bigger, resembling large bombers with wings constructed of painted sheet metal or a Goodyear sign with spinning propellers and landing gear extended for touchdown on the tarmac. Many of these early pieces are adorned with ducks, made of diamond plate steel or thick sheet metal, painted in green and red and accented with reflectors. One duck, attached to a form that resembles a deconstructed airplane, is enormous with an eight-foot-long body and six-feet-long steel rotating wings, all covered in road signs cut in various shapes and patterns. It makes for a striking color palette that sparkles and glows when reflecting the headlights of passing cars at night. In those early years Vollis lined six pieces up near the shop and scattered another fourteen or so pieces around a fence line that rims a pasture enclosing a small fishing pond.

Vollis's work seemed to build toward an apex of two monumental pieces that lend voice to his skills as a mechanic and engineer, his honed use of recycled materials, and his prodigious talent as an artist. The first is a 4,500-pound, 55-foot-long cacophonous assemblage of bicycle wheels, stainless steel sheet metal, HVAC fans, stainless steel stove pipe, planes turned from wooden sign posts, textile mill rollers, aluminum cups, school bus mirrors, a bicycle frame, circular roof vents, sheet metal, truck hubs, and road signs cut and shaped into stars, triangles, rectangles, and fan blades to cover every available surface. Unique among Vollis's sculptures are the letters cut from white road signs and attached to a diamond grate frame spelling out in all capital letters his signature: V. SIMPSON. The piece has more than sixty-five moving parts, making it seem alive, perpetually moving and spinning as the arrow-shaped vane turns the massive German steel (with attached plaque in German) frame into the wind. Although none of the spinning fans create a secondary motion as a whirligig is defined, the sheer size and amount of clanging, twirling parts, and pieces attached to the frame is overwhelming to the senses. The complexity of the piece and its profile, which seems sparse and simple viewed from the side and maddeningly dense observed from the end, demands deep inspection to understand how the sculpture is even assembled.

It is harder to understand (at least for me, and I knew Vollis personally) how one man could create something so amazing. The more I have thought about it, it's no wonder that he signed the sculpture; if I had made something as brilliant as V. SIMPSON, I would have signed it, too.

When Vollis would talk about his whirligig *The Horses*, he said it was the only one of his pieces he needed help erecting out in the pasture. Because it was so heavy, it required a bigger pole than the other whirligigs, and the pole it was mounted on need to be deeper than all the other poles—fourteen feet deep. So instead of breaking out the hole digger with extensions attached, digging the hole by hand, pouring cement, and setting the pole into the ground like he did for all of the other pieces, Vollis hired a well digger and a crane to set the piece and had concrete poured around the pole to set the whirligig in place. This piece is special. It's not the tallest, it doesn't have the most moving parts, and it doesn't have the biggest diameter wheel, but it stands out among all the other whirligigs Simpson made. It's massive in overall size, with a front wheel that is striking for its demure color choice, white with relatively little adornment. Originally it had four large fans attached to the front wheel before Vollis switched them out years after it had been in the field for a couple of dozen smaller HVAC fans, which he mounted on the wheel with rollers he bought in bulk from the salvage yard. But the front wheel and the fans attached are just a small part of this piece. Behind the wheel, Vollis used an old cotton gin drive that he modified to transfer the movement from the front wheel to the vane of the whirligig. But he didn't construct a traditional wind-catching vane; instead, he assembled wheels, wood, metal, reflectors, and other parts and engineered them into a kinetic vane that instead of just turning the whirligig into the wind, turned the wind into a storyteller. *Horses* consists of a team of mules (Vollis called them "the mules" or "the horses"; he made them as mules, although many saw them as horses) that simply pulls a wagon, although the engineering and mechanics that he put into the piece make it special. When the front wheel engages the drive, the drive moves the legs on each of the mules, while also wagging the mule ears. As the beasts walk forward, the wheels on the wagon spin and the man perched on his bench seat at the front of the wagon moves his arm in a motion that mimics the light whipping of the mule team, pushing them forward on their journey. The effect is that the entire piece seems to be moving forward while stationary in the air.

There is a playful elegance about *Horses* that is comforting. The piece isn't abstract; it's the opposite—grounded in the time and place that Vollis grew up, where he moved buildings with his father or worked the farm with a team of mules. One day when I was out visiting Vollis, I heard from the locals about the significance of the piece and its placement at the back of the field near the pond. These guys had grown up farming in the area and were doing some work for Vollis, clearing brush around the pasture one afternoon, when we began talking. Before long the conversation turned from idle chit chat to a discussion about the whirligigs, and one of the men started telling me about working on the farm with Vollis and his family. He said that *Horses* brought back his childhood. When he was young, he had unloaded many a guano sack off a mule wagon at the same spot where Vollis had raised his sculpture. To him, that's why Vollis made it and placed it in that spot, as a kind of memorial to those times years ago when farmwork was more brute force and less mechanization. Vollis's whirligigs are not just abstract, figurative, or even historical sculptures; they are pieces of a puzzle that tell a much greater story of people, land, and community.

Over the years many have referred to the pasture and the whirligigs contained within as Acid Park, a name that is connected to a local legend that says Vollis built the whirligigs, mounted them in the pasture, and covered them in reflectors because he was mourning the loss of a daughter who passed away in a car accident. Some say Vollis was attempting to recreate the last trippy high of his daughter and her boyfriend before they crashed, or maybe he was sending a warning, bright and intense, so no one else would succumb to the hot rod curves of rural Wiggins Mill Road. Some said that Vollis himself was the one that was high and crazy. (Contrary to the rumors, his daughter is alive, with kids of her own, and his sons are alive, and his wife, Jean, still lives in the house where Vollis was born.) Instead, I've always thought that Vollis was smarter than most folks and with his wealth of commonsense ability and technical skill, he creatively built what he could imagine and built it bigger than most folks could easily wrap their minds around.

There is an element of whimsy in what Vollis built, a playful conversation that I think many people see in his work, that bares his soft side, which was a large part of who he was. But more and more, the whirligigs are for me that conversation that gets to a place I hadn't expected, a depth to what he was making out of scrapped metal, fiberglass, wood, copper, aluminum . . . parts and pieces crafted and shaped and welded and painted into a collection of stories, a long conversation. He was open to learning, to seeing that anything and everything, any piece of material, however neglected by others, might be important: whether it was an absurdly long and large steel pipe, dozens of spindles out of an old closed-up cotton mill, hundreds of HVAC fans in seemingly every possible size and shape, a big plastic hot pepper from a Chili's restaurant, an old heating oil drum, a Federal WLR Fire Truck Siren, a 1930s Ford Wide Five Hub and Wheel, electroplated nickel silver wine goblets, roofing tacks, threaded rod, milkshake cups. Each piece of material carried its own stories, and Vollis had the talent and skill to mold them into new shapes and forms to tell another story, a different story that revealed what was inside him and the culture of the community of which he was a part. His sculptures, whirligigs, and windmills spoke a language that people understood.

As Vollis grew older and began to slow down, we often spent days doing more talking than working. Vollis lived with his art and taught me more than once as a friend. Many times, the things that work best aren't necessarily glossy, new, and shiny, but are a little older, used, even worn-out, and can often get the job done better. I miss Vollis and those times we sat around and talked about life and windmills, but I still have him around every time we repair and conserve one of his older whirligigs so they can be mounted in downtown Wilson for the opening of the Vollis Simpson Whirligig Park and Museum. When it does open, on the former site of one of Wilson's old brick tobacco warehouses, I know that Vollis will live on through what he created and a new generation will learn about engineering, mechanics, physics, science, technology, and conservation through the art that he started making that day he decided to put all of that scrap material up in the pasture.

DAVID HOUSTON

The Art of Welmon Sharlhorne

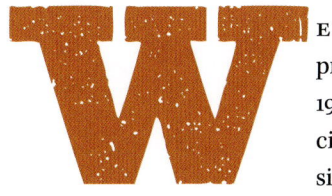ELMON SHARLHORNE is an artist who continues to produce work against all odds. Born in New Orleans in 1952, Welmon grew up in the country just south of the city in Houma, Louisiana. Rural, deeply segregated, and sitting at the very edge of where the continent meets the Gulf of Mexico, Houma offered little opportunity for the young and uneducated, especially African American young men. Welmon drifted from odd job to odd job, and then into petty crime, which landed him in a juvenile detention center near Baton Rouge, Louisiana, for four years. After a few short months of freedom, Welmon was once again in trouble with the law and graduated from juvenile detention to the infamous Angola prison in North Louisiana where he spent over two decades serving time for a series of burglary and extortion charges.

While in Angola, Welmon was taken with the urge to make images and began a series of highly imaginative drawings with common markers on paper and manila folders that he continues today. As with many self-invented artists, Welmon's work is quirky and individualistic and consists of a singular iconography related to events close to his daily life: walled buildings, cathedrals, doing time, the thirst for freedom, and the monsters within. Barely able to write his own name, making art was a literal and conceptual leap for Welmon, but one that transformed his life. Finding a larger sense of purpose, art making has kept Welmon focused through his prison years and the hardscrabble life he led living on the streets of New Orleans after his release. When I first met Welmon in 2001, he carried his entire world contained in a black briefcase and hanging in a few laundries around New Orleans. In spite of being homeless, hungry, and penniless, Welmon has a distinct sense of pride, and indeed a sense of calling, in being an artist that has allowed him to rise above the dire circumstances in which he has lived.

Welmon's early prison works were ink on manila folders made with a series of found templates to form the tight geometry of his drawings. This basic geometry was invigorated by imaginative variations of a few often-repeated themes and an innate talent

Welmon Sharlhorne, *Red Tree with Bus and Monster*, courtesy of the artist

for all-over decorative patterning. Welmon's work, in his own words "made it out of prison before he did" and was valued by dealers and collectors for his meticulous, detailed rendering, inventive subject matter, and exotic style before he became known as an artist and a New Orleans personality. Although undocumented due to his illiteracy, Welmon is also a wordsmith, often summarizing a long conversation with a rap-like poem of the major points of discussion or telling moral tales to young people through rhyming poetic narratives.

Welmon Sharlehorn's work is included in important collections such as the Smithsonian American Art Museum (Washington, DC), Collection de l'Art Brut (Lausanne, Switzerland), and the American Visionary Art Museum (Baltimore, Maryland). His life and work are included in most of the major publications about contemporary self-taught artists. Over the past few years, Welmon has settled into a shotgun house in the Treme neighborhood of New Orleans but may still often be seen walking the streets of the French Quarter.

ERIN LEE ANTONAK

Healing Art

BOTH OF MY PARENTS died and were revived before I was born. My father overdosed on heroin at age fifteen, and my mother drowned when she was four. My mother used to tell me that her spirit flew above her body and she could see herself in her brown dress before anyone found her. She said she looked like a brown paper bag floating in the pond.

I grew up surrounded by chaos.

During the week my extended family would make crafts. On weekends we would pack up our conversion van and head to powwows where we would set up our craft table and put on our regalia to dance. We often traveled with my maternal grandfather. My grandfather was a member of the False Face Society and of the secretive Little Water Society, a medicine man, soothsayer, woodcarver, and the last traditional chief of our tribe. He would bring me to ceremonies, teach me to make things, and tell me stories about what it was like to grow up as a healer. When he was dying, I got a rare chance to experience the ancient ceremonies that are performed only for people considered to be of great spiritual importance.

I left home at fifteen years old. I attended college, traveled, and landed in New Orleans. New ceremonies took place in my studio and in galleries. Instead of making ceremonial regalia and *gustoweh* headdresses, I used the same skills to make hats and costumes for drag queens and burlesque dancers.

When I was twenty-five years old, my mother had a massive brain hemorrhage that left her paralyzed from the neck down, and my father resumed his opiate addiction. The healers arrived from Canada to take care of my mother after one of them had a vision about her. She, too, became a Little Water member, like her father, the ceremony taking place right in her hospital room. This brought me back to my home and the ceremonies of my youth. Twelve years later, I lost my father two weeks before the birth of my first son. My mother died ten days after the birth of my second.

I have never known a ceremony that was designed for my personal brand of pain and grief. I have never discovered a ritual that accurately addressed my hope and joy.

Erin Lee Antonak, Untitled, courtesy of the artist

I have never found one religion, spiritual practice, or belief system that gave me comfort and made total sense to me. I feel this is true for so many people. I think so many of us are searching for something to help us, fix us, comfort us.

When I was a girl, I would braid cornhusks into long ropes that my mother would sew into *gad jeesa*, husk face masks, to be used in ceremony. Women in my family have done this for many generations. As we braid, we pray, and our prayers and our powers are put into the braids so the masks, when completed, can come alive and heal.

I continue to make objects that heal. Working on them allows me to do *something* when there is nothing more reasonable to be done. The repetition in my work allows for the same meditative process that braiding does. In this way, the making of these layered objects and the drawing of repetitive images is healing for me. I see my finished works as cultural artifacts, remnants of ambiguous ceremonies and rituals.

DAVID HOUSTON

The Art of Leo Twiggs

L EO TWIGGS's "We Have Known Rivers" series is born of the confluence of personal history, African American heritage, and contemporary events. Inspired by Langston Hughes' poem, "The Negro Speaks of Rivers," "We Have Known Rivers" builds on Twiggs's personal iconography of ancestral faces, nature, and the undulating lines of rivers. The artist sees waterways as the vessels of African American experience—ancient, past, and present. A great many of Twiggs's African ancestors were intimately intertwined with agriculture, both in Africa and in the so-called "New World." Agriculture was inextricably linked to water as sources of nourishment, growth, and transportation.

In this body of work, "We Have Known Rivers," Twiggs presents a tripartite composition of earth, sky, and water inhabited with faces and people that reference both the artist's legacy and the contemporary world.

Twiggs works in a batik technique, a process that he developed after several years of experimenting with the traditional medium. Batik is a way of making images with pigment on wax resist, used mostly for decorative arts in Indonesia, Africa, and ancient Egypt. Twiggs was a pioneer of using batik in the United States as a narrative high art form.

NOTE
Special thanks to Hampton Gallery III and Sandy Rupp in Taylors, South Carolina, who represent Leo Twiggs.

Leo Twiggs, *Connections* from the *We Have Known Rivers* Series, Collection of Winston-Salem State University, courtesy of the artist

Edward Rice, *Meadow Garden*, courtesy of the artist

CULINARY KINSHIPS

JAKI SHELTON GREEN

i know the grandmother one had hands

i know the grandmother one had hands
but they were always in bowls
folding, pinching, rolling the dough
making the bread
i know the grandmother one had hands
but they were always under water
sifting rice
blueing clothes
starching lives
i know the grandmother one had hands
but they were always in the earth
planting seeds
removing weeds
growing knives
burying sons
i know the grandmother one had hands
but they were always under
the cloth
pushing it along
helping it birth into
skirt
dress
curtains to lock out
night
i know the grandmother one had hands
but they were always inside
the hair
parting
plaiting

twisting it into rainbows
i know the grandmother one had hands
but they were always inside
pockets
holding the knots
counting the twisted veins
holding onto herself
lest her hands disappear
into sky
i know the grandmother one had hands
but they were always inside the clouds
poking holes for the
rain to fall.

BILL SMITH

Grandmother's Cooking/

Cuisine de Grand-mère

I DON'T THINK OF MYSELF as sentimental or nostalgic, but having said that, I confess that almost every day I look back to inform my work. For many years I found myself trying to bring the good but simple food of Eastern North Carolina to the diners at Chapel Hill's Crook's Corner. I grew up in a time when large families were still the norm. Like as not, these families were run by matriarchs. Ours on my mother's side of the family was my great-grandmother Inez. She was a fantastic cook and hardly a day passes when I don't think back on something she made.

I paid a lot of attention to cooking as a child. This was way before it ever occurred to me to be a chef. (I *was* sometimes called upon to assist. For instance, if I produced four cups of wild blackberries or perfect pecan halves, there would be a pie.) At my grandmother's table, food was a serious topic. Endless discussions of country butter versus store bought; arguments over seasoning; backhanded compliments about skills. Without even realizing it, I was learning a point of view that shapes me as a professional chef today. Good food. No nonsense.

Hard crab stew is one of those favorites that I had not brought to the restaurant because it is so messy to eat. It's a summer stew, eaten outdoors on tables covered with newspapers. It has rituals. We probably only had it twice a summer. Once in grandmother's garden and once during the week when we took a house at the beach. In those days, we caught our own crabs, so it could be quite a production for that reason alone. All you need is a chicken neck on a string and a scoop net. It is a stew that is eaten with the hands as much as with a spoon. There is a slice of white bread in the bottom of every bowl. Don't make fun. I served it to a group of friends at the Outer Banks last weekend and their bowls were clean.

I finally began serving a more refined, less messy version of hard crab stew at Crook's Corner and public events. Below, however, is the original. Nut crackers help you get to the meat. Use the claw shells to dig it out. Most people only have patience enough for a crab or two, but it's the broth that counts—along with the slice of white bread.

Recipe for Hard Crab Stew

Serves a crowd

½ pound side meat or fatback

2 medium onions, peeled and cut into large dice

2 dozen hard crabs, cleaned and halved

½ teaspoon crushed red pepper flakes

4 bay leaves

1 teaspoon thyme

6 baking-sized potatoes, peeled and cut into eighths

¾ cup all-purpose cornmeal, stirred into two cups of cold water

Salt and pepper to taste

Sliced grocery store white bread

Render the side meat in a large stockpot. Do this slowly, as it has a low smoking point and you want to extract as much fat as possible before it gets too brown. It will resemble crisp bacon in color when ready. Add the onions and sauté until soft but not brown. Add the crabs and cover with cold water. Add the red pepper, bay leaves, and thyme. Bring to a boil, then turn back to a simmer. Cook for half an hour, and then add the potatoes. Cook until they are well done, fifteen to twenty minutes more. Turn up the heat a little (but you don't want a hard boil) and stir in the cornmeal and water. This will be a little difficult because of the crabs. You need to mix this in thoroughly. Bring back to a simmer until the stew begins to thicken. Taste for salt and pepper. Sometimes the side meat will be saltier than other times.

To serve, put a slice or two of bread in the bottom of large soup bowls and ladle the stew, crabs and all, on top. Claw crackers would be handy. We used to get yelled at for cracking the claws with our teeth.

PETER MABLI

Whole Hog, Partial Acceptance

The Problematic Commensality of Fourth of July Barbecues in the Antebellum South

OW THAT THE temperature is rising in the Northeast and I begin the annual tradition of rolling my Weber grill back onto our patio, I am reminded of the complex and problematic history of barbecues in the United States. I can't help it: such bubble-bursting thoughts are a frequent side effect of studying history. In the following excerpt from my dissertation, "'I Choose to Sit at the Great National Table': American Cuisine and Identity in the Early Republic," I detail some of the social and racial inequities inherent in barbecue feasts, particularly Fourth of July celebrations that praised the benefits of American independence while simultaneously ignoring certain oppressed and enslaved populations. My intent with this passage is not to ruin anyone's Fourth of July weekend, but I do hope to give you pause to reflect on the underlying cultural implications of celebrating our seemingly benign holidays and traditions. Enjoy your hot dog!

Fourth of July barbecues were important cultural celebrations in the early American Republic that highlighted the young nation's attempts to form a communal identity. The obvious correlation between patriotic acts and the celebration of national independence aside, Fourth of July celebrations also instilled the concept of a shared American identity through the incorporation of large, festive, and lavish feasts to commemorate the occasion. Primarily in the southern and western states, a community barbecue became the symbol of the supposed abundance and convivial nature of American society. Yet these celebrations also ironically exposed deep-seated cultural hierarchies that ultimately revealed a nation divided and at odds with its own celebrations of unity and independence.

The American minister Charles A. Goodrich detailed the cultural significance of barbecue and its impact on American nationalism in his 1836 travelogue, *The Universal*

Traveller. "Among the amusements of the people of the Southern States," he wrote, "we find the Barbecue, and it is generally [considered] . . . an act of hospitality." Goodrich described how gentlemen from throughout the region would chose to "unite for the purpose" of roasting "some savoury animal whole . . . after the manner of the ancients."[1] The spirit of unity and community inclusiveness was evident in Goodrich's review of the event, but more importantly, so too was the connotation and connection of the barbecue to American Indian society. His passing reference to the "manner of the ancients" alluded to the origins of the practice of barbecuing: a practice first observed and recorded by European authors in America as early as the sixteenth century.[2]

Open-flame roasting was of course a cooking technique almost universally practiced, but the specific spit-roasted, whole-animal methods of Native peoples were of great interest to early European colonizers. By the mid-nineteenth century, the practice had become deeply ensconced in American national society even as the word "barbecue" itself remained associated with Native populations and cultures.[3] A slow process of dissociation from American Indian cultures and appropriation into European society began early, however, and ultimately helped to distance barbecues from their supposed native origins. Goodrich's passing reference exemplifies a cultural and intellectual evolution of the cooking practice away from its indigenous provenance and toward a supposedly unique American style.

American author and traveler Charles Lanman reiterated this evolutionary dissociation in 1850 when he (incorrectly) asserted that the word barbecue was in fact not American Indian in origin but rather "derived from a combination of two French words signifying "*from the head to the tail,* or rather according to the moderns, *the whole figure, or the whole hog.*" Lanman conceded that, "By some, this species of entertainment is thought to have originated in the West India Islands." Without any proof, he concluded it to be "quite certain that [barbecue] was first introduced into this country by the early settlers of Virginia" and the considered practice, "commonly looked upon as a *pleasant invention* of the Old Dominion." Europeans and later Americans desperately tried to culturally remove themselves from the people whose cooking styles and methods they had adopted, going as far as to invent false origin stories to help bolster their arguments. The process of cultural appropriation seemed to come full circle in subsequent passages of Lanman's work, as he concluded that a review of the practice of barbecuing "deserves more praise than censure, as we know of none which affords the stranger a better opportunity of studying the character of the yeomanry of the Southern States."[4] Thus, over the course of a couple generations, barbecue went from being an exotic American Indian cooking practice indicative of the supposed barbarism of indigenous peoples, to a peculiar Old Dominion invention, one that positively affirmed the cultural identity of white Americans in the American South.

Such cultural appropriation in the era was predicated on the appealing nature of barbecues both as a savory meal and an effective means to build community and influence political culture and elections. Following the War of 1812, Democrats seized upon the practice of large-scale celebratory barbecues as a means to unite the people and sway elections. As Andrew Jackson's biographer Robert V. Remini describes, "Nothing beats food and drink to capture the interest of the American electorate. Even when the Democrats lost elections they seemed to think a barbecue was in order."[5] The irony of celebrating Andrew Jackson—an infamous opponent of American Indian peoples—with a culinary tradition originating from American Indian nations was seemingly lost on the populace.

Regardless of the origin of barbecuing and the motives of its participants, the practice had become fundamentally associated with specific components of white American society by the 1820s. Descriptions of barbecues were filled with hyperbolic statements and weighty prose that spoke to the supposed grandeur and beauty of American society highlighted in these communal feasts. In his journal, the famed American naturalist John James Audubon detailed a barbecue in Kentucky in such a manner. "As the youth of Kentucky lightly and gayly advanced towards the barbecue," he wrote, "they resembled a procession of nymphs and disguised divinities. Fathers and mothers smiled upon them as they followed the brilliant cortège." The barbecue in question was a celebration of Independence Day, and on this day, Audubon felt "Columbia's sons and daughters seemed to have grown younger that morning."[6]

Audubon's description of the Kentucky Independence barbecue addressed a number of tropes that had come to define the positive qualities of American national character. The event was an egalitarian affair, full of great energy, optimism, and a sense of communal pride. "The whole neighborhood joined with one consent," he described, "no personal invitation was required where everyone was welcomed by his neighbor, and from the governor to the guider of the plough all met with light hearts and merry faces." That all members of society (from "the governor" to the "guider of the plough") were gathered at the event was an important component of Audubon's description of American social egalitarianism. Further, the need to define community through nationalism in his passages was uniquely required in the western states, as questions regarding the ability of the nation to remain unified as its boundaries expanded remained an ever-present concern of the era. Audubon addressed these concerns by describing these "bold, erect" Kentuckians as "proud of their Virginia descent," and pleased to "make arrangements for celebrating the day of [their] country's independence."[7] Therefore, even out west, Americans remained united through their shared political and cultural heritage.

Audubon continued by describing the food at the event as varied and plentiful and detailed how each participant in the barbecue "had freely given his ox, his ham, his venison, his Turkeys [as well as] melons of all sorts, peaches, plums, and pears [that] would have sufficed to stock a market. In a word, Kentucky, the land of abundance, had supplied a feast for her children."[8]

As they ate their meals, the participants sang the praises of their founders, further connecting the convivial meal with the American nation. The speeches, according to Audubon, "served to remind every Kentuckian present of the glorious name, the patriotism, the courage, and the virtue of our immortal [George] Washington." As was customary in many large feasts of the era, toasts were also made to similar American political figures and national sources of pride. "Many a national toast was offered and accepted," Audubon wrote, "many speeches were delivered, and many essays in amicable reply." As the event came to a close, Audubon reveled in the scene he had witnessed. The barbecue had such a profound effect on the author, he concluded his "spirit to be refreshed every Fourth of July by the recollection of that day's merriment."[9]

While colorful and poetic, Audubon's description of a Fourth of July barbecue was far from unique. As early as 1803, the *Hornet* newspaper publicized a "Republican Barbecue" to be held outside of Woodsburgh, Maryland. "It would be unnecessary," the paper argued, "to describe the satisfaction, peace, and friendly intercourse that subsisted at this numerous and respectable meeting." The paper continued by describing the event as a meeting of a "Band of Brothers," with members "old and young—rich and poor—a meeting of freemen," further exemplifying the supposed egalitarianism of American society.[10] The event also included a toast to numerous patriotic people and ideas, including the president of the United States, the political concept of republicanism, and a toast against traitors such as Benedict Arnold and—not surprisingly for a Democratic-Republican event—John Adams.[11]

However, barbecues were not relegated only to the southern states. A Fourth of July barbecue was planned for Madison, Wisconsin, in 1843 and described by the local paper as "evidence of the taste, beauty, good cheer, and patriotic ardor" of the town.[12] After the usual set of toasts and patriotic songs, the paper proclaimed the attendees would "partake of the numerous excellent viands, rarities, and delicacies . . . prepared by the united liberality of the citizens of Madison."[13] Although the festival occurred in one of the northernmost towns in the country, the Madison Fourth of July barbecue remained surprisingly similar in tone and procedure to its southern equivalents. The unifying nature of such celebrations was seemingly easy to replicate throughout the nation. Indeed, barbecues remained the quintessential method of celebration in the early Republic, fusing the burgeoning American national cuisine with the ideals of the developing American political and social culture.

Regardless of the barbecue's perceived inclusive nature, however, these celebrations of freedom through commensality remained stolen from the practices of an oppressed native population, and—equally disturbing—were often prepared in the southern states by the enslaved. For instance, in the engraving accompanying a description of Virginia barbecues, Samuel Goodrich's travelogue alluded to the fact that Black slaves lit the barbecue pits and cooked the meals for their white masters. In the visual, a Black man and woman are seen turning a whole hog on a spit while another young Black man stirs a pot near the fire. White men dressed in formal attire relax under a tree and play cards while a group of white women and children dance in the background. The master/slave relationship was in full effect in the visual, yet Goodrich did not mention this fact in his written account. In contrast, Audubon did mention enslaved people in the description of the Kentucky barbecue he witnessed. In passing, Audubon wrote that "for a whole week or more many servants and some masters had been busily engaged in clearing an area [for the barbecue]."[14] But beyond this observation, Audubon never returned to discuss the further actions and impact that slaves had on the day's festivities.

Regardless of the lack of references in these accounts, it is clear that slaves held important roles and responsibilities in southern barbecues. On large plantations as well as in private homes, enslaved African Americans often generally served in culinary roles as food cultivators and chefs, and it is logical to assume that they took their knowledge and practices in daily meal preparation and applied it to barbecue festivals. Louis Hughes, a former slave who recounted his enslavement in Virginia in his memoir *Thirty Years a Slave*, described in detail the intricate barbecue cooking practices of enslaved cooks:

> The method of cooking the meat was to dig a trench in the ground about six feet long and eighteen inches deep. This trench was filled with wood and bark which was set on fire, and, when it was burned to a great bed of coals, the hog was split through the back bone, and laid on poles which had been placed across the trench. The sheep were treated in the same way, and both were turned from side to side as they cooked. During the process of roasting[,] the cooks basted the carcasses with a preparation furnished from the great house, consisting of butter, pepper, salt and vinegar, and this was continued until the meat was ready to serve.[15]

The barbecue style was indeed a complicated process, one that took many years to master and came with a generous amount of admiration within the slave community. Beyond the slave quarters, this cooking practice was also often well respected. Hughes described how it was common knowledge in the southern states that "slaves could barbecue meats best," and consequently, "when the whites had barbecues, slaves always did the cooking." Nevertheless, the power dynamics and social structure of slavery were certainly not forgotten during a barbecue, and even if there was a short moment of levity and celebration during the feast itself, it was merely, as Hughes wrote, only "a ray of sunlight in [our] darkened lives."[16]

The juxtaposition of Independence Day celebrations prepared by enslaved peoples represented one of the starkest cultural contrasts inherent in food culture in the early American Republic. In most respects, the convivial nature of these and other public feasts was undercut by their ability to expose underlying injustices in American society. The inability to reconcile—and at times even to acknowledge—these issues in certain written descriptions spoke to the fundamental prejudice and inequality that pervaded American society. By the turn of the nineteenth century, Americans had shed their postcolonial identity in favor of a stronger national sense of self. But what Americans implemented nationally in its stead exposed inherent complications and contradictions in their society. In this new system, food and cuisine remained a symbolic representation of the American people, both for good or ill. And in Fourth of July barbecues of the era (culinary practices appropriated from oppressed native peoples and prepared by enslaved populations) the colorful nationalistic language and haughty calls for unity that accompanied the communal feasts and festivities often rang hollow for large swaths of the population.

NOTES

1. Charles A. Goodrich, *The Universal Traveller, Designed to Introduce Readers at Home to an Acquaintance with the Arts, Customs, and Manners, of the Principal Modern Nations on the Globe* (Hartford: Canfield & Robbins, 1836), 39.

2. For a detailed description and observations of early barbecuing in North America, see Andrew Warnes, *Savage Barbecue: Race, Culture, and the Invention of America's First Food* (Athens: University of Georgia Press, 2008).

3. In his work, Warnes details the complex history of the concept of barbecue—including its associations with Native Americans and savagery—and also describes the inability to easily ascertain the etymology of the word itself. Often the word is attributed to the Arawakan phrase *barbacoa*, meaning "a roasted animal." But there is also a connection to the general concept of *barbarism* that European colonizers associated with native peoples. "Barbecue mythology arose," Warnes writes, "neither from actual Arawakan life nor from any other indigenous culture, but from loaded and fraught colonial representations that sought to present those cultures as barbaric antithesis of European achievement." Warnes, *Savage Barbecue*, xxii.

4. Charles Lanman, *Haw-Ho-Noo; or, Records of a Tourist* (Philadelphia: Lippincott, Grambo, and Co., 1850), 94, 97.

5. Robert Remini, *Andrew Jackson: The Course of American Freedom, 1822–1832* (Baltimore: Johns Hopkins University Press, 1981), 382–383.

6. John James Audubon, "A Kentucky Barbecue," in *Audubon and His Journals*, edited by Maria Audubon (London: John C. Nimmo Press, 1843), 487.

7. Audubon, "A Kentucky Barbecue," 488.

8. Ibid., 487.

9. Audubon, "A Kentucky Barbecue," 488.

10. "A Republican Barbecue," *The Hornet* (Frederick, MD), October 25, 1803, 1.

11. Ibid.

12. "Fourth of July," *The Wisconsin Democrat* (Madison, WI), June 22, 1843, 2.

13. "Fourth of July," *The Wisconsin Democrat*, 2.

14. Audubon, "A Kentucky Barbecue," 487.

15. Louis Hughes, *Thirty Years a Slave: From Bondage to Freedom* (Milwaukee: South Side Printing Company, 1897), 49.

16. Ibid., 50, 51.

KATERINA KATSARKA WHITLEY

The Flavors that Bind Us

I N THOSE EARLY YEARS, the cultural shocks were almost as frequent as the fried chicken dinners. I had left an exuberant extended family in Greece to study in the American South. Decades later I came to recognize that the transition from my high school, Anatolia College of Thessaloniki, to a small college in North Carolina was a mercy; a large university would have been too much of a shock for a sheltered girl of sixteen. Even so, the differences could have defeated me had I not been young, optimistic, and surprisingly resilient.

I had grown up in a city surrounded by familiar faces, a watcher and an observer. We didn't enclose ourselves in cars, so we walked everywhere in the central streets of Thessaloniki. Venizelou Street, named for the finest statesman modern Greece produced, took me to Egnatia Street, known by St. Paul and the evangelist Luke. I climbed to what had been the Turkish part of the city to see my grandparents and admired the fifteenth-century White Tower at least once a week at our waterfront. History enveloped me. On those walks, I saw the same faces, recognized them on the evening promenades, and knew who belonged to which *parea*, the in-group that always moved together. Our apartments breathed through their balconies, and there we sat in the late afternoon, watching the people passing by, knowing their style of dressing, the peculiarities of their walks. I suspect that those watchful hours were the first hints of the writing to come.

I was rarely alone; eating by myself would not have occurred to me. The meals were communal experiences: tasty offerings, scintillating conversations, laughter, and arguments.

Then, suddenly, with very little preparation, I found myself in a country where air conditioning isolated families in the summer, and cars cocooned them from one place to the other in the winter. I had gone from a European city where everyone seemed visible to small-town America where neighbors were miles away; from historical research and beloved myths covering twenty-four centuries to a near veneration of Civil War mementos.

I became even more of an observer. Mystified, I tried to find a key to this new country, something to connect me and remind me of home. The closest I came was at church, where the hymns and prayers were familiar to this Protestant Greek. But church was too organized, too limited by time constrictions. Even church, such an intimate part of my childhood, was not home.

During breaks and holidays, I was invited to people's homes. I would like to pretend that I remember the meals they offered, but the only ones that come to mind are fried chicken with mashed potatoes, roast beef with vegetables, and the occasional cookout with the tantalizing aroma of steaks or hamburgers on the grill. Conversations were subdued and arguments nonexistent. In the quiet that enveloped the table, I wondered what would help them digest their main meal, which in the South those days, was eaten at midday. It was called dinner, not lunch. And after they ate it, they did not lie down for a siesta! Strange.

In the small southern towns of the 1950s, foreign-tasting dishes with exotic names would have been an oddity had they been offered, but they simply were not. Although I missed so much, I found many customs I did admire. The hospitality of my southern hosts reminded me of my own Greeks. Eating at least one meal a day as a family was a habit that was honored in the homes I visited. I liked being greeted by people I passed by on campus or in the street, people I didn't know, just because their natural friendliness said, "I acknowledge you." Undergirding all this was an unfailing politeness. Years later, when I traveled widely in the United States, I recognized that these good manners and friendliness were not necessarily as American as they were southern.

Iced tea was sweet and a new experience for me. Coffee was rather terrible. Hush puppies were interesting, biscuits comforting, bacon a new and welcome taste. Finishing a meal with dessert instead of fruit was a temptation I could have done without, but a hot apple pie with ice cream did not have its equal back home.

In the 1960s, in my own home in the United States now, I invited neighbors and guests to sample new dishes. The question of a young woman who asked, when I offered her spanakopita, "Are these collard greens?" became a neighborhood joke. Feta may have smelled strong to those who had never eaten any cheese beyond Velveeta, but as an accompaniment to my flavorful fresh green beans, it was a huge success. At church suppers my beans, with olive oil, onions, tomatoes, parsley, and dill, became famous. In the American South I was using Greek flavors but still longing for flat-leaf parsley, phyllo dough, and leeks.

When did the 1980s arrive, and when did they disappear? All of a sudden there were packages of phyllo dough in local supermarkets, Kalamata olives became a staple, and a rather poor version of feta cheese was sold, hermetically enclosed in plastic. What a gift these were to someone like me who lived in towns where I was perhaps the only

Greek, the one who loved to invite guests for an extended dinnertime. Friends and guests succumbed to the new tastes I offered and sought out Greece herself, the country, the land of incomparable beauty. It was inevitable that when American tourists returned home they wanted to taste again the tzatziki and souvlaki they had enjoyed in Greek tavernas.

I enjoyed cooking for a small number of friends, but my husband, proud of my cooking, urged me to invite enough people to fill the living spaces. So I produced *papoutsakia*—eggplant halved and stuffed with meat sauce and topped by béchamel and feta; *psari mayonnaiza*—bass cooked and served cold in a mold of potatoes, carrots, capers, and homemade mayonnaise; *dolmathakia*—rice wrapped in grape leaves; and countless variations of layered pitas. Even though I never ate baklava in restaurants or bought it in shops (no Greek thinks another's baklava is good enough), I made my own, and the lightness and aroma of it delighted my guests. Friends commented that in my home there was a perfect blend of Greek flavors with an overlay of southern hospitality and manners.

It was obvious that food, the sacrament of breaking bread together, was the tie that bound me—a thoroughly Greek woman—to my new home, the American small-town South. It was inevitable that I would start remembering my childhood kitchen, its aromas and ambiance, and in the remembering I would both cook and write. One time, I dared to challenge the North Carolina supremacy of barbecuing pig and anointing it with vinegar. The essay I wrote for the Raleigh *News and Observer* made a big splash, and my fellow citizens would bring it up whenever we met. One friend, a farmer, stopped me on my way to the post office and said, "I will provide the pig, if you do the cooking." I laughed and said, "Make sure it's small."

So I invited twenty-five or so friends and started the preparations. We dug a hole in the yard and another friend supplied the hickory wood for the fire. He even offered to do the turning of the spit. I showed him how the Greeks skewered the whole dressed pig lengthwise and his job was to turn it and baste it with lemon juice whipped with olive oil and oregano. Among many Greek dishes I made a salad of large butter beans cooked in my own sauce; for the starters, baked *tyropitakia,* triangles of phyllo with a filling of feta, yogurt, eggs, and dill weed; and roasted potatoes in lemon and oregano. That meal was eaten nearly thirty years ago. A friend from those days who now lives near me in Louisville, Kentucky, still talks about it with loving nostalgia. For me, those hours spent cooking and serving were a gift; it was as if I were living in a Greek village sharing my cooking with those who crowded its square. A delightful blend of two cultures has sustained me through the decades, and my life has been enriched by both.

A recipe to accompany my story

The one recommendation I have for roasted pork meat is to use the simplest flavors: olive oil whipped with lemon juice for basting; oregano or thyme may be added together with salt and pepper. To accompany this, I offer potatoes, which are a hit wherever and whenever I serve them. These earthy flavors complement each other beautifully.

Patates to fournou, riganates

Peel and slice lengthwise six potatoes, Yukon gold or russet work the best. When serving a lot of people, figure one potato per person. The potato slices should be at least twice the size of what you would use for French fries.

Preheat oven to 400 degrees.

Wrap potato slices in a clean towel to dry them as much as possible. Place them in a large baking pan or an iron skillet. If you are serving many potatoes, you may need two pans because they do better spread as a single layer. Sprinkle olive oil on them and toss them until the potatoes are glistening with the coating. Then sprinkle the juice of a whole lemon on them. Salt and pepper them and add a tablespoon of dried oregano. Toss them so the herbs and lemon juice bless them sufficiently.

Place potatoes in the hot oven and bake for at least half an hour. Taste one for tenderness. The potatoes should be crisp on the outside and soft inside. If you want crispier slices raise the temperature to 450 and watch them carefully. Serve them with slices of lemon.

A green salad and crusty bread are all you need with the pork and potatoes. But if you want to add a green dish, try this.

Summer string beans

2 pounds fresh green (string) beans
1/2 cup good olive oil
1 medium onion
3 large ripe tomatoes, peeled and shredded or 3/4 cup crushed tomatoes
1 teaspoon sugar
2 heaping tablespoons of fresh snipped parsley and equal fresh dill
Salt and pepper to taste

String beans are tender and plentiful in the summer. Prepare two pounds of fresh beans by snipping off the stems and washing them in cold water.

In a deep heavy pot, pour 1/2 cup olive oil. Slice and chop one medium onion and sauté in the olive oil until translucent. If you have ripe tomatoes, peel three large ones and chop them before adding them to the onion. Add a teaspoonful of sugar and salt and pepper to taste. Stir. Add the beans and enough water to almost reach the top of the beans. Cover, bring to a boil, and then lower the heat. Keep them partially covered. The length of cooking will depend on the freshness of the beans, from half an hour to a full hour. You want the water to be absorbed so the sauce is red but not watery. (If all the water is absorbed before they are done, add a bit more water.) Ten minutes before removing from heat, add two heaping tablespoons of snipped fresh parsley and two more of fresh dill. The beans are done when you can cut them with a fork. Serve with good feta.

Elizabeth Matheson, *Coolmore, Tarboro, NC*, courtesy of the artist

SOUTHERN AFTERLIVES

JOHN JUNG

To Live and Die in the South

The Chinese Story

NTIL THE LAST third of the past century, there were few Chinese immigrants in the Deep South. By the 1870s, a handful of Chinese immigrants began fleeing from the violence they encountered on the Pacific coast to find refuge in small towns throughout the US South. Almost all were young or middle-aged men seeking a way to earn a living, send money back to impoverished families in China, and eventually return to China. Most of these Chinese operated hand laundries or small neighborhood grocery stores.

Life in the racially segregated Jim Crow South presented challenges for the Chinese as they were neither black nor white. Given that they were the only, or one of a handful of, Chinese in the towns where they settled, there were no Chinatowns where they could work and live as found in places such as New York City or San Francisco. They generally lived and worked in poorer parts of town where the rent was low.

If they died, where could they be buried? Being so few in number, they could not afford to finance a cemetery for Chinese only. In towns where only a few Chinese lived, there might be no need for a cemetery because there were no deaths over many decades. It is possible that in these circumstances, a Chinese who died might be buried in either a Black or white cemetery without opposition. In 1890, H. Leon, the first Chinese, or "Celestial," as they were usually referred to in newspapers, to die in Atlanta was buried in a white cemetery following funeral services held at an Episcopal church. In contrast, according to Reverend Ted Shepherd who ministered to the Chinese in Greenville, Mississippi, for many years, early Chinese decedents were buried in an African American cemetery, Live Oaks.

Mississippi had a large number of Chinese scattered up and down the Delta region with only a handful in most towns. Greenville, in the heart of the Delta, was unique in creating a small cemetery in 1913 for Chinese only. When a need for more space arose, the Chinese Cemetery Association purchased 5.8 acres in 1931 for $1,000 donated by Chinese businesses and some of their wholesalers to replace the original Chinese cemetery. It provided a resting place not only for Chinese who died in Greenville but also for those who died in other Delta towns.

The Delta Chinese adorned the cemetery with aspects of Chinese culture and beliefs. A pagodalike structure serves as the central entrance. A spiked iron gate that could be locked with a chain was needed to thwart acts of vandalism that occurred occasionally in the past. On a marble slab on the left side of the main entrance is a poem in Chinese that depicts the soul resting in heaven on a clear night with a bright moon. The soul is thinking about and enjoying memories of home and family. On the right side of the main entrance the poem goes on to state that this place is quiet and peaceful and asks, *why not be satisfied where you are?*

There are two additional entrances on either side of the central entrance. Each of these entrances has a sun symbol on a post on the left side to represent day or life while a star symbol on the post on the right side represents night or death.

New Orleans has the largest number of Chinese buried in the South. One section of a white cemetery, Cypress Grove, holds a Chinese tomb, dedicated in 1904 by the Soon On Tong Association for the burial of its own members. Tongs were fraternal organizations that provided vital services to the early Chinese, including job placement, immigration services, Taoist shrines, and gambling facilities as well as funeral arrangements and the transportation of remains back to China. The Chinese tomb held many decedents in its fifty-two vaults that occupied four levels of two wings. New Orleans is below sea level so caskets had to be placed above ground due to the dangers of flooding. An older Chinese tomb dates back to the 1890s in the historic St. Louis No. 1 Cemetery behind the French Quarter. In the 1960s, the On Leong Association built a third Chinese tomb in Greenwood Cemetery. There are at least another hundred Chinese family tombs in the city.

Chinese, like other immigrants in New Orleans, built society tombs that held more than one descendant to lower costs. The front of the tomb included an enclosed worship space, an altar, and a spirit tablet, inscribed with the name of the deceased in the center, their ancestral hometown, and the names of any surviving children and grandchildren.

Early Chinese were typically buried in a temporary grave because they came as sojourners with the intent to eventually return to China to be reunited with their families when they could no longer work. If they died before they could return, many wanted their bones buried in China. Several years after the burial, the remains would be exhumed, cleaned, packaged, and shipped to China.

In Augusta, Georgia, for example, eight Chinese bodies were disinterred from cemeteries in 1919 and sent to Atlanta to be prepared for shipment to China. It was noted that these men had received Christian burials in Augusta, but they would receive Confucian rites in China before being placed in their final resting place. By the 1930s, however, this practice waned as more Chinese felt less need to be reburied in China because they had succeeded in bringing their families over or had established new families here in the United States. World War II, followed by the rise of Communist China in 1949, further discouraged plans for reburial in China.

In cities with many Chinese, decedents were buried in a section of a white rather than a Chinese cemetery. Magnolia Cemetery in Augusta is a white cemetery, but Chinese could be buried there. Greenwood Cemetery, a white cemetery in Atlanta, has a section where Chinese are buried that is enclosed on three sides by an iron-pipe rail fence. An obelisk some thirty feet tall rises in the center of the section. The inscription at the base reads Chee Hung Tong, Chinese Free Masons, September 8, 1911, and recognizes the Chinese benevolent organization that provided for the space. The decedents were not all from Atlanta but included Chinese from as far away as Chattanooga, Tennessee, who wanted to be buried near other Chinese. Elmwood, a white cemetery in Memphis, also had a section for Chinese burials.

Headstones of many, but not all, graves are inscribed with the names of the decedents in Chinese characters with or without their American names as shown in the marker from the grave of Wong Kam Chen in Augusta, Georgia. His father, Wong Yoke Hing, was buried in the same grave sometime in the 1920s, but around 1930 his remains were exhumed and returned to China. His son died soon after and since his father's grave was then conveniently vacant, he was buried in it.

The practice of placing names on tombstones in Chinese characters is important because Chinese names often did not match their American names. The Chinese Exclusion Act, in effect from 1882 to 1943 to prevent the admission of Chinese laborers, led many Chinese to purchase identity documents that bore names of the documents' original owners rather than their own names. For example, someone whose clan name was actually Chan might have to use a different surname over his lifetime if the surname on his identity document differed from his real name. However, after he died, his grave marker would bear, in Chinese characters, his true surname, Chan. Names of decedents written in Chinese characters on tombstones have proved invaluable information for accurate tracing of family histories.

Chinese Funeral Customs

A Chinese funeral involves an elaborate set of rituals that were invoked if there was a large Chinese community. Chinese in the South, due to their small numbers, were limited in the extent to which they could follow traditional customs. Even so, there was no difficulty in following the custom of providing arriving mourners with two symbolic tokens: a piece of hard candy and a nickel. The candy served to provide a sweet taste to ease the bitterness of sorrow and the coin represented hope for prosperity. At the end of the service, guests received a small red envelope or *lai see* containing a quarter so that they might buy more candy. In contrast, the traditional ritual of having a small marching band leading a procession of mourners behind the hearse after the funeral service as it passed by the decedent's residence or place of business for a brief pause was impossible in places with small Chinese populations. At this site, a family member would remove a black ribbon bow from the door that the funeral director would then place on the casket, symbolizing that the spirit of the deceased had left the home to join the body for the "long journey." The procession would resume its way to the cemetery for the burial after which the family hosted a longevity dinner for the guests at a Chinese restaurant.

Qing Ming Rituals

Chinese all over the world pay respect to deceased relatives during the Qing Ming spring ritual also known as Tomb-Sweeping Day. This traditional Chinese festival occurs on the first day of the fifth solar term of the traditional Chinese lunar calendar. The literal translation of Qing Ming is "clean and bright." On this day each year Chinese sweep the graves of their ancestors. The festival is an important ancestor worship ritual in which families clear weeds around the tomb and add fresh soil to show their care of the dead. They place offerings of favorite foods of the deceased at the grave along with paper resembling money. This is all burned in the hope that the deceased will not lack food and money. Incense is burned and prayers are offered. In contemporary Hong Kong, Chinese also burn paper imitations of mobile phones, laptops, refrigerators, air conditioners, and even luxury cars.

Westerners who typically brought only flowers to the gravesite were surprised and even amused by the Qing Ming rituals of Chinese as illustrated by this 1895 Atlanta newspaper account describing Chinese customs at the Westview Cemetery.

> A peculiar part of the exercises was that the offerings were all set at the foot of the deceased, and the menu offered for the delectation of the particular deity whom they wished to honor was of the choicest viands so fondly cherished by the Chinese.
>
> At the foot, on either side of the grave were placed two small candles of red . . . between these were arranged three little bowls filled with boiled rice . . . three tiny cups of fragile and beautiful design were arranged in a row in front of the rice bowls. These cups were filled with whisky. Next came a roasted fowl, a huge pieced of boiled pork, three chopsticks, and then a profusion of apples, pears, and bananas.
>
> Each member of the party, with one exception, approached the foot of the banquet table, and after making various signs of his utter unworthiness to partake of

the good things, took up one of the cups, and, after sprinkling its contents about the feast, refilled his cup, and with a final salaam made way for the next. . . . At the conclusion of these ceremonies a huge pile of varicolored papers was set on fire . . . it was thought that the party would leave the whisky . . . but they did not do so for they put the liquor back and left everything else.

Over time, Chinese in the South practiced the traditional rituals less extensively as in the past, especially later generations of descendants who adopted Western practices. Edward Wong, who grew up in Augusta, recalls that during Qing Ming his family would visit the grave of his cousin Wong Kam Chen. Other Chinese families would also gather at the cemetery during Qing Ming to pay respects to their deceased relatives. Afterward, they would all depart in a procession to visit two other nearby cemeteries where only a few Chinese were buried. Chinese today still uphold the spirit of Qing Ming to honor one's ancestors even though most of the newer generations, especially those born in the South, have adopted Western funeral customs.

ANDREW FARRIER

St. Louis Cemetery #1

T 9:15 A.M., as the crowd gathers, it's easy to see that not everyone anticipated how hateful the morning sunlight would feel. Visiting a cemetery is one of the linchpins of a good trip to New Orleans, and the oldest and most popular is St. Louis Cemetery #1. Our early start time minimizes the chance that someone will faint in the subtropical heat. The cemetery is a labyrinth of white tombs that reflect sunlight and is surrounded by brick walls that block the breeze, with only a handful of palm trees for shade. But the prospect of an early morning rarely deters ambitious travel planners as they envision their adventure from afar.

But the famous spontaneity and liveliness of a night in the French Quarter doesn't mix with optimistic, premeditated, prenoon plans. Those who do show up often bear signs of where they were a few hours before: squinting eyes, a half-washed stamp on the back of a hand, or a fresh Bloody Mary. We meet one block from Bourbon Street, and plenty of guests cross it on their way to find me, seeing, perhaps with horror, how little the sun flatters the street that looked so seductive under moonlight and neon. Those who don't see it can still smell the transformation the rising heat wreaks upon the stagnant remains of parties past along that notorious walk. Whether you slept or not, the ghost of last night is inescapable.

For me as their guide, it's important to engage them and give them a reason not to regret waking up—or not going to sleep at all. Luckily, my easiest conversation starter is something I genuinely wonder about: What inspired you, in a city known for its nightlife, to set an alarm, ooze out of bed, and visit a cemetery?

A few are eager to share—an elderly woman once confided that as a girl she had fallen in love with local playboy Bernard de Marigny (d. 1868) and had been inspired to whitewash his neglected tomb; now she wanted to see him again. For most, however, the idea that cemeteries are creepy seems to shadow the question, and to avoid seeming creepy themselves, they start their answer with a sheepish smile or some other form of hemming and hawing. Some are clearly more excited than they can comfortably express. As a gay man, I feel a mixture of sympathy and excitement for these particular guests. Serious death enthusiasts are a stigmatized minority, and with any such group there is a need, at some point, to come out of the closet. Confident, quiet comfort with oneself is an ideal place to land, but in the initial, clumsy catapult into openness, few hit that target squarely. Many undershoot the mark; they giggle when I ask what they're excited for, and then, perhaps in a harsh whisper, utter, "Marie LaVOO," reverently mispronouncing the name of the famous voodoo priestess. Some overshoot the mark, grinning at my question and saying, "I'm just a freak," reclaiming the slurs used against them as badges of honor. They are, of course, talking to a professional cemetery tour guide, who, reflection would suggest, probably shares their enthusiasm, but accustomed loneliness makes for a guard that doesn't come down easily. Our tour, I hope, can be a step toward ease for them.

A few months into my tour guiding tenure, I got the first really arresting response to my question: one woman, with a Harley jacket and a ready smile, answered that she was a professional mortician and that she taught mortuary science at a university. As an eager but untried new arrival to death-related professions—I wasn't even aware that mortuary science was the established term—I began to feel the mix of dread and excitement that means I'm about to learn a lot. However, she quickly put me, as well as the rest of the group, at ease; she clearly loved her job, her knowledge was fascinating, and her lightheartedness contagious.

After the tour, the mortician and I exchanged contact information, and our correspondence culminated a few months later when I visited her campus and gave a presentation on New Orleans cemeteries during the annual professional development meeting of the Michigan Embalmers' Society. Popular psychology suggests that public speaking and death are the human race's greatest fears; on this occasion I got to face both simultaneously, along with a third one that for me outweighs the others: the fear of appearing ignorant. I'm used to an audience of death neophytes beside whom I'm a relative authority, and here, the tables were turned. This was never clearer than during the tour she gave me of their department. The rooms and devices and fluids she named were foreign and, honestly, a bit terrifying, driving home the fact that when the time came for my talk, only my extremely niche knowledge of New Orleans burial would defend me from being the most ignorant person in the room. It also did not escape me that I would be the only person present who had never handled a corpse. I tend to feel my nervousness in the soles of my feet, and they were screaming in my blue suede shoes as I walked to the podium.

The event itself was predictably anticlimactic. The undergrads were quiet, like most undergrads, but the adult professionals were warm and engaged, had thoughtful questions, and continued the conversation over lunch—the best tour group I could imagine, minus our thousand-mile separation from the cemetery. My ride back to the airport came as a favor from one of the students, a laid-off autoworker who had used the loss of his job to go back to school. He said he was happy with his choice—being a mortician, he explained, felt like a more examined and truer fit for him than the least-resistance option of working for an auto manufacturer. He also mentioned one of the most common answers to my pre-tour question: he said he had always loved horror movies. But he said it with a smile and no embarrassment.

That trip added new stories and facts to my playbook, and I often joke about the framed certificate of honorary membership in the Michigan Embalmers' Society that hangs on my wall. But it was also the first time I had seen a large gathering of people who shared an interest in death and felt no shame about it. And I concluded that my new acquaintances in Michigan were experts at something at which many of my cemetery tour guests are beginners: attaining comfort with morbid curiosity.

I won't call it luck, but chance soon provided me an opportunity to observe morbid curiosity in a new way. There was an outbreak of vandalism in St. Louis #1. Defacing of the tombs was nothing new, people have been drawing x's on tombs they think house voodoo practitioners for decades at least, scratching them in with coins or staining the plaster with lipstick and sharpies. Late in 2013, though, shortly after I returned from Michigan, a vandal countervandalized the tomb of Marie Laveau against the aforementioned vandalism—painting the large monument bright pink and obscuring the thousands of x's beneath. This made the news in town and got the tomb a $10,000 renovation.

Then, in the spring of 2014, St. Louis #1 made the news again. While leading a tour one day, I saw a familiar tomb that looked different since my last visit: a brick was missing from its façade, the square of its absence offering a view into the interior darkness. A man stood before it whom I recognized as one of the unlicensed tour guides who scrounged odd dollars by soliciting confused tourists inside the cemetery. I watched as he gathered his group around the tomb, took a camera from one of his guests, stuck it and his hand through the hole, and returned it to her with the added weight of a flash photo that, judging by her expression, she was not eager to see. He was arrested before long.

Perhaps inspired by the publicity, imitators appeared, scraping the soft mortar from numerous tombs and leaving some with small peepholes—others fully exposed to the air—with bottles and garbage at the back to suggest people had put more than a hand inside. That outbreak prompted the archdiocese to close the cemetery to the public, only allowing family members and groups escorted by approved tour guides to enter. Now, the gates are guarded. After making headlines three times in less than a year, the cemetery has been quiet for months; aside from three huge x's drawn in blood on the side of Marie Laveau's tomb one morning, I haven't seen new vandalism since.

Like my jaunt in Michigan, these stories made their way into my tour. The tomb with the missing brick stands near another damaged monument, this one with a large hole at its base, caused not by vandalism, but by nature: a palm tree grew out of it and fell over. Pointing out and explaining these back-to-back, I see radically different responses: to vandalism, disquiet or disgust; but to natural, chance exposure to the inside of a tomb, fascination. Below the age of about fourteen, kids rush to look inside. Older folks are more inhibited; some calmly ask whether there are any human remains inside, others ask it with a nervous chuckle, and still others back away from the opening, their feet retreating while their eyes rivet on the hole. What I almost never see is indifference. Attraction and revulsion are there in different ratios, but feelings are consistently strong. Never mind that there are no bones within—the empty hole is enough to evoke the absent body, and the sight of nature taking its course is enough to release morbid curiosity that elsewhere might be restrained.

I tell this story at least once a week, and I'm conscious of pieces missing from it. I never asked the arrested man what inspired him to become an unlicensed tour guide. Demand probably played a role—like me, he was paid for his services. But I can conceive of a story where he came to it by way of a passion—the love of something that becomes a means of making a living by happy accident. Maybe he visited and vandalized the cemetery out of a personal fondness for seeing and handling the hidden dead that could be fulfilled no other way, and maybe he chose St. Louis #1, as popular as it is, from a love of risk or exhibitionism that came back to haunt him. That would be the southern gothic scenario, if an unlikely and gratuitous one.

I can conceive of this story because mine was similar. I grew up in St. Francisville, Louisiana, a small town that local tradition claims started as a cemetery. In the 1790s the community stood along the Mississippi and flooded every spring. They buried their dead on a nearby bluff to keep them from washing away, and after enough floods, the living decided that they deserved the same dignity. That original Catholic cemetery is still there, alongside its younger Episcopalian neighbor, each a mix of headstones and mausoleums, and as kids, my friends and I would explore them. We would feel the worn inscriptions, thrilling at early dates (any birth date in the 1700s felt like a glimpse into the Big Bang) or cool names (Savannah Lana or Solomon Wisdom). Once we discovered a crumbling brick mausoleum at the edge of the woods. A thick iron door, rusty and crooked but clearly functional, stood on one side, secured with a padlock. Brickwork had once concealed its contents from view, but time had opened a hole above the door, just large enough to look inside. As with the palm tree tomb in St. Louis #1, there was no body to see, but there was more than just absence, too—behind the door, a steep stairway led down into what looked like an underground tunnel of about human height. It was impossible from that vantage to see how far the tunnel went.

We were not apt researchers, and for a long time we preferred making up stories to investigating. Once we began to ask around, the stories we heard varied around a general thrust: long ago, a young man had reacted to his wife's unexpected death by constructing a special tomb where he could visit her in the solitude of an underground chamber. We heard and repeated this story until one of us had the insight to ask at the historical society. The docent disagreed—the story, she said, was a legend. In reality, the structure was never a tomb, but a Civil War hideout disguised as a tomb, meant to be used as an emergency shelter for civilians should the town see sudden battle. No one knew, she told us, whether it had ever been used, but the Episcopal church had been shelled during the war, and the tomb may well have saved lives.

Around this time, after years of hoarding stories, my friends and I got hired to share them as tour guides at the Myrtles Plantation. It being famously haunted, the demographic we met brought the same morbid curiosity I see today as well as, a delight in being scared. We learned to recognize this trait—they tended to laugh after they gasped—and established a small business on the side. If we hit it off with a tour guest, we might offer to bring them on a nighttime visit to the cemetery. Plenty of the house's former inhabitants were buried there, and the church and cemetery were left unlocked all night. Those who accepted would accompany us on the short drive into town, and we would escort them through the creaking cast-iron gate into the cover of the oak trees, whose leaves and moss would eclipse the moonlight. By flashlight we would show them the graves, simply and professionally. There was no need to work at scaring people under these conditions.

The last and optional part of our time in the cemetery was a visit to the Civil War hideout tomb. We would describe it from afar and offer to bring them there, on the understanding that it was at the edge of the woods in the darkest part of the cemetery—nothing would be visible outside the flashlight's beam, and they might hear a coyote howl in the woods. If they said yes, then one of us, agreed upon beforehand, would bow out—to go to the bathroom, we'd say. When it was me, my job was to run toward the front of the cemetery, but then, once out of sight, I'd circle the church and beat them to the tomb. The shifting of its foundation had opened a hole in the earth on the side opposite the door, through which it was possible to slide into the underground chamber; once I found the hole, I'd drop in, feet first, from darkness into blackness. From there I would climb the stairs and wait behind the door until I saw the flashlight's beam approach. If I timed it right, my hand could emerge from the hole, clawing at the door, exactly as they got close enough to look inside. We were close enough to the woods that no one would hear when they screamed, or a moment later when, if we'd chosen right, they laughed.

For years I've shared this story when people ask me why I became a cemetery tour guide. There are tight parallels between me and the unlicensed guide in St. Louis Cemetery #1 for sure. We both satiated morbid curiosity for pay by putting our bodies into tombs, and a much larger percentage of the body in my case. But my story is easy to tell lightheartedly—even tourists love a story about a prank played on an unsuspecting tourist, and since the monument we invaded wasn't actually a tomb, it's easy to see it as harmless fun. This remained the case until a friend of mine in New Orleans decided to visit St. Francisville on her own. After seeing the Civil War hideout tomb, she paid a visit to the historical society to see what she could learn. She came back with news: the Civil War hideout story, the docent had told her, was a legend. In fact, she had claimed, the structure was a tomb where a man had buried his prematurely lost bride so that he could visit her beneath the ground. In this light, my story loses some of its levity.

Here I have to overcome my discomfort with ignorance. Either story might be true, or both. Both sound simultaneously believable and fantastical. I might have ignorantly entered a tomb, or I might have consciously entered a tomblike non-tomb. The same story told those two different ways could make a listener feel disgust or fascination. And so I might be more like the vandals in St. Louis #1 who knocked a tomb open, or I might be more like the palm tree that grew and fell, knocking a tomb open. When I finish my tours today, I tell them this story, and I tell it with all the ambiguity in place. The mystery makes for a better story than any of the possible certainties, and if the listener, confronted with that mystery, laughs about death, then I feel like I've done my job well.

LYNN YORK

A Visit from the Bereavement Committee

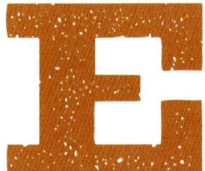 VERYONE HAS FEARS about death—loss of control, pain, leaving loved ones behind, regret, eternal damnation. As a daughter of the South, however, I hold yet another overriding horror: a visit from the bereavement committee. Let's be clear, it's not death I fear—it's the committee.

For those who don't belong to a church somewhere in the southern United States, a bereavement committee is a group of well-meaning and generous women who descend on the household of a deceased person, providing comfort, food, and labor. Feeding, cleaning up, and looking after a mourning family is a high calling. Someone brings ham, of course, and there are casseroles. In certain quarters, there is a little competition to see just who can get their food to the bereaved the fastest. Some people precook their bereavement meals and store them in their basement freezer chests. I consider this cheating, and also a little creepy. Others would say, death is part of the circle of life, and it's best to be prepared.

It's this very preparedness that makes me wary. I am the epitome of unpreparedness. I have never come upon a tragic occasion in my life with a serviceable pair of pantyhose in my possession. It is only now that pantyhose have gone out of style that I can attend a funeral without a big run up my leg. It stands to reason also that I will die in a state of unpreparedness, very much like the young woman in my mother's church who died suddenly and unexpectedly. The bereavement committee arrived to find a sink full of dishes, eight or more loads of dirty laundry (*filthy* dirty, according to all reports), and not even an ounce of milk in the refrigerator for those poor motherless children who undoubtedly had dirty necks and not a decent outfit among them to wear to the funeral. So, not only did this woman die, but then everyone in town heard about her dirty carpets.

As a decent, progressive southern woman, of course, I hereby disapprove of the bereavement committee and their judgment of this woman. She died, and her children and her household needed support, not a makeover. However, in the dark night of my soul, I shudder. I remain mortified for this woman. For several weeks after hearing this tale, I made sure to wipe down the counters and sweep the floor before turning in, lest I died before I woke.

I am aware that my fear of judgment, especially over my housekeeping, is horribly unliberated. I am working on it, I assure you. However, I was raised by a woman who had to clean the house for a week before I could have a sleepover. We ate every single meal on a placemat with a fork, knife, and spoon sitting in their proper arrangement, even if we were eating baloney sandwiches.

If you come to eat at my house, I will probably not put the bottle of ketchup on the table. I will put ketchup in a little bowl and hand it to you like that's the way we always serve it. There is still part of me that wants to iron my cloth napkins. In truth, most of them are stained and stashed in a basket in my laundry room at this moment, hidden from the bereavement committee. However, I do aspire to iron them, so that upon my death, a committee member will find them, pressed and sorted by color in the drawer of my buffet, right beside my recently polished silver.

I do not really understand this compulsion for prissy perfection, but I fear that there is a little of the bereavement committee in me as well. It is the same craziness that drives me to pretend that I have my Christmas shopping done in November. I will also tell you that I'm having a great day even if I want to wallow on the floor with depression. I will beg you to stay for dinner even though I hate you and have only two pork chops and a box of rice. I can also swear that I have never emitted a bodily odor or had one too many glasses of wine. Because, really, I rarely drink. There is no need for any member of the committee to go into the bottom cabinet of my butler pantry because those bottles there, they are just for entertaining. They've been there forever. Honestly.

If there is an upside to all of this southern-lady pretense, it's that it leads us to our real friends. A real friend is the person with whom you can drop all of the BS. You can put the ketchup bottle and the liquor bottle right on the table, pour your friend a drink, and then you can tell her just how bad you are feeling. She will never tell a soul. This intimacy is our reward for having to face the bereavement committee all of our lives. In fact, a real friend will not only deny any and all nasty rumors about you; if you should die suddenly, she will sprint over to your house, wash all your dishes, burn your journals, and iron your napkins before the first member of the bereavement committee walks into the door. Friends, I am this woman. Call me if you die. I'll do the same.

Kendall Shaw, *Sunship, for John Coltrane*, courtesy of the Ogden Museum of Southern Art

JAMES PEACOCK

Afterword

SOUTH WRIT LARGE is a labor of many loves against a history of some hates, regional, national, and global, as well as an account of some of the impressive energies deployed to understand and redeem them. Here are a few of the efforts and persons involved.

Howard Odum led Franklin Roosevelt to bring the New Deal to the US South. He did so in part by writing an influential book, published by UNC Press in 1936, *Southern Regions of the United States*. My late brother-in-law, Sam Hay, a cattle farmer, lived a mile away from where Odum grew up, in Newton County, Georgia. I once asked Sam about Odum. He said that in the South many were suffering in poverty and Odum helped Franklin Roosevelt to understand that. That understanding helped bring about the New Deal. Odum's sons, Tom and Gene, who pioneered in ecology, carried on his legacy, and the granddaughters of his nephew, Junior Odum, sheriff of Newton County, are the young actresses Elle and Dakota Fanning.

Far from Odum in time and place, other figures emerge. In the South, of course, there were the Agrarians at Vanderbilt University, who honored the southern tradition. At the far end of the world, on the island of Java, there was a young woman, Juker Tati Imam Muhni, part of the royal family of the Sultan of Yogyakarta, a kingdom established in the 1700s as the Dutch conquered Java. She read William Faulkner avidly and then won a fellowship to study southern literature at the University of North Carolina. Returning to Yogya, she created an excellent program in American Studies at the University of Gadjah Mada, and sent some of her students to Carolina, one of whom is today a leader of the Muhammadiyah, one of the largest Muslim organizations in the world.

Back at UNC, Dan Patterson built a superb program in folklore which, among other things, adopted Tati as an emerging folklorist who did field research and published a book on bingo in Maryland. At that time, and perhaps still, the most distinguished scholars of the South were, at Carolina and beyond, in the fields of history and literature, notably Louis Rubin, as well as in sociology in the Odum tradition, notably John Shelton Reed.

I arrived at Carolina in 1967, coming from Princeton where I had helped establish a department of anthropology, and was soon going with Dan Patterson to horsetrading and other events. Then I met Ruel Tyson, who had just come back to North Carolina from Texas and Chicago to join the Department of Religious Studies. He, Dan, and I, in company with our spouses, notably Beverly Patterson, did research among the Primitive Baptists in the mountains and Pentecostals in the lowlands for many years. Tati helped sustain and build my abiding interest in Indonesia, which led to a global focus as well, now flourishing through scholars like writer Samia Serageldin, who is a scholar of the South and is also deeply rooted in Egypt.

David Moltke-Hansen came to Carolina to head the immense Southern Historical Collection, and his leadership soon prompted a revival and extension of southern studies. He and I co-chaired a meeting at Wilson Library in 1989 that resulted in the creation of the Center for the Study of the American South (CSAS).

Not long after the creation of the CSAS, a major step was taken toward globalism at Carolina. In 1993, which was the two-hundred-year anniversary of the opening of Carolina's doors to Old East in 1793, Craig Calhoun founded UCIS, the University Center for International Studies. Many grants were won and projects created. When Craig left to head the Social Science Research Council in New York, Provost Richardson asked me to become director of UCIS, in which capacity I served until 2003. Bogdan Leja remained on the UCIS staff, and I recruited Raymond Farrow and Niklaus Steiner. We continued many of the projects and developed new ones, while also planning a building, which was approved and is now the FedEx Global Education Center, which has honored me by naming the atrium after Florence and James Peacock. Arthur Deberry and Marguerite Hutchinson led the effort to so name the atrium. Hutchinson and her son also led in developing the current site of CSAS, reminding us of a link between CSAS and FedEx, i.e., of "Southwritlarge." Incidentally, that name was supported by Patrick Inman, active in the early development of the magazine by that name.

From the start, we envisioned a synergy between local and global, symbolized by an acronym, GLOBGRO or "grounded globalism." We worked in partnership with CSAS, the Institute for Arts and Humanities, and many other schools and programs, including conferences with Professor Lothar Honighausen at the University of Bonn, who is a scholar of William Faulkner. The proceeds of these conferences were published by the University of Wisconsin Press, and I wrote a book, *Grounded Globalism: How the U.S. South Embraces the World* (2007), published in the New Southern Studies series of the University of Georgia Press. Ruel Tyson and I partnered in a conference at the Friday Center that focused on the synergy between southern and global understandings. The conference was funded by the Rockefeller Foundation, drew several hundred participants, and won an award as an outstanding conference. Also noteworthy was the creation of the Sonja Haynes Stone Center for Black Culture and History, with whom we collaborated, especially during the directorship of Joseph Jordan. Finally, we created a seminar, the Global South Group, or "South Writ Large," which continues to meet and has resulted in numerous publications and other spinoffs, including the *South Writ Large* online magazine.

In sum, *South Writ Large* reflects some years of creative, productive work and thought reflected in the online magazine by that name and now in this anthology, edited by the magazine's editors, in alphabetical order: Amanda Bellows, Katherine Doss, Robin Miura, and Samia Serageldin. Let us congratulate the writers and editors as well at UNC Press for ushering into life this superb and timely collection of brilliant and relevant writings about the South Writ Large.

CONTRIBUTORS

ERIN LEE ANTONAK is a sculptor, a milliner, and a Wolf Clan member of the Oneida Indian Nation of New York. She holds a BFA from Bard College, an MFA from SUNY New Paltz, and has studied at Lacoste School of the Arts, France, and Vermont Studio Center. Erin has worked in various museums and art galleries developing, designing, and building exhibitions for more than twenty years. She has organized and curated shows in Europe, Asia, North America, South America, and Africa. Her artwork fuses traditional Iroquois sensibilities and craft techniques with contemporary materials and concepts. She is currently the curator at the Ohr-O'Keefe Museum of Art in Biloxi, Mississippi, the board chair of the Indigenous Women's Voices Summit, Hurleyville, New York, and serves as a Yale University Morse College Fellow. She lives in Ocean Springs, Mississippi, with her husband, Brian, and their children, Calder and Archer.

BO BARTLETT is an American realist with a modernist vision. Bartlett was educated at the Pennsylvania Academy of the Fine Arts, where realist principles must be grasped before modernist ventures are encouraged. He pushes the boundaries of the realist tradition with his multilayered imagery. Life, death, passage, memory, and confrontation coexist easily in his world. Family and friends are the cast of characters that appear in his dreamlike narrative works. Although the scenes are set around his childhood home in Georgia or his island summer home in Maine, they represent a deeper, mythical concept of the archetypal, universal home (taken from *Bo Bartlett, Heartland* by Tom Butler).

TARLETON BLACKWELL is a native of Manning, South Carolina. A 1978 graduate of Benedict College in Columbia, South Carolina, Blackwell received both an MA and an MFA from the University of South Carolina. In 1990, he earned an associate of science degree in funeral service from Gupton-Jones College of Funeral Service in Atlanta, Georgia, and is both a nationally licensed funeral director and embalmer. He is former manager, funeral director, and embalmer for Blackwell and Jenkins Funeral Home in Manning, South Carolina. From 2002 through 2006, Blackwell was a visiting professor and artist in residence, holding the Martha Beach Endowed Chair in Painting at the University of North Carolina at Pembroke. He is former art instructor for Florence School District Two, Clarendon County School District Two, South Carolina State University, Williamsburg County Schools, the Columbia Museum of

Art, the South Carolina Governor's School for the Arts, and Vermont College of Norwich University. In 2018, he retired from his teaching career as the art instructor at Scott's Branch High School, Clarendon School District One, in Summerton, South Carolina. Blackwell has been named an "Outstanding Young Man of America" and an "Outstanding Professional South Carolinian in the Field of Art." His website is www.tarletonblackwell.com.

PAULETTE BOUDREAUX's novel *Mulberry* is the winner of the inaugural Lee Smith Novel Prize from Carolina Wren Press (now Blair). She is a Mississippi native currently living in Los Gatos, California. She is a member of the MFA faculty at the Mississippi University for Women and has published short stories and novel excerpts in national and international literary journals. She has a bachelor's degree in journalism from Northeastern University and a master's in fine arts from Mills College.

W. HODDING CARTER III is an award-winning journalist, educator, public official, and civic leader. Born in New Orleans, Louisiana, raised in Greenville, Mississippi, and educated at Princeton University, he began his journalistic career in 1959 as a reporter with his family's Pulitzer Prize–winning *Delta Democrat-Times* in Greenville and went on to become its managing editor and associate publisher. During his tenure, he was active in the civil rights movement as an editor and in political action. He worked for two successful presidential campaigns, Lyndon B. Johnson's in 1964, and Jimmy Carter's in 1976. President Carter appointed him Assistant Secretary of State for Public Affairs and spokesman for the State Department, where he became the public face for the administration during the Iran hostage crisis. He went on to a national career in the media as television commentator and newspaper correspondent on public affairs, working with ABC, NBC, CNN, PBS, BBC, and the *New York Times,* among other leading media, and in the process earning four national Emmy Awards and the Edward R. Murrow Award for his documentaries. He served as the Knight Professor of Public Affairs Journalism at the University of Maryland from 1994 until he resigned to serve as president of Knight Foundation, a position he held from 1998 to 2005. Carter is a retired professor of leadership and public policy at the University of North Carolina at Chapel Hill. Among his publications are *The Reagan Years* and *The South Strikes Back.*

KAREN L. COX was born in Huntington, West Virginia but has lived in the South ever since, including stints in Mississippi and Kentucky. Now a professor of history at the University of North Carolina at Charlotte, she's written numerous op-eds for the *New York Times*, *Washington Post*, *CNN*, *Time*, and *Smithsonian Magazine* and is the author of four books, including *Dixie's Daughters: The United Daughters of the Confederacy and the Preservation of Confederate Culture, Dreaming of Dixie: How the South Was Created in American Popular Culture, Goat Castle: A True Story of Murder, Race,* *and the Gothic South*, and *No Common Ground: Confederate Monuments and the On-going Fight for Racial Justice*.

JEFFERSON CURRIE II is an enrolled member of the Lumbee Tribe of North Carolina and a native North Carolinian. After graduating from the University of North Carolina at Pembroke with a BA in American Indian studies, he worked for more than ten years at the North Carolina Museum of History in Raleigh as a curator, historian, and researcher for exhibits and educational programs. Jefferson completed the coursework for a master of arts in folklore at the University of North Carolina at Chapel Hill, and after grad school, for many years, he served as the daily repair and conservation manager for the Vollis Simpson Whirligig Project in Wilson, North Carolina. Currently, he is the Lumber Riverkeeper, charged with protecting and maintaining the water quality of the watershed so that it has clean fishable, swimmable, and drinkable waters.

NAJEE DORSEY is a visual artist and entrepreneur. As an artist, Najee Dorsey has developed in his craft over the years and has become known for his mixed-media collage, digital media collage images of little-known and unsung historical figures, as well as nostalgic scenes from African American life in the southern United States. In his work, as Najee chronicles moments in Black life throughout history, he maintains that "stories untold are stories forgotten." Najee founded Black Art in America™ (BAIA) in 2010 as a free online media platform for African American artists, collectors, art enthusiasts, and arts professionals. BAIA™ was founded as a centralized location for profiling the African American artist—giving members of the network access to the work of African American artists (past and contemporary) and, most importantly, opportunities for interchange. Since 2010, the network has become the leading online portal and resource focused on African American art, artists, collectors, industry leaders, and arts enthusiasts. More information on the artist can be found at www.najeedorsey.com.

JOHN P. DUNN entered the world in Wiesbaden, in what was then West Germany. He has traveled to Europe, Africa, and Central Asia but lived longest in his favorite town: Valdosta, Georgia. Currently a professor of history at Valdosta State University, he offers courses dealing with the Middle East, Eastern Europe, China, and world military history.

ANDREW FARRIER is a writer and performer based in New Orleans, Louisiana. Besides appearing on camera and occasionally on stage, he also presents audio fiction and audio stories about queer history and shares New Orleans history and present-day stories on YouTube. You can find all this and more at www.andrewfarrier.com. He still shows folks around cemeteries in New Orleans and remains a proud honorary member of the Michigan Embalmers' Society.

RICHARD GRANT is an author, freelance journalist, and television host. He grew up mostly in London, England, and now lives in Mississippi. He writes for *Smithsonian*, the *New York Times*, *Garden and Gun*, the *Guardian*, and many other publications. His nonfiction works include the adventure travel classic *God's Middle Finger*, about a lawless mountain range in Mexico, and *American Nomads*, a history and memoir of wanderlust in North America. He wrote the southern bestseller *Dispatches From Pluto: Lost and Found in the Mississippi Delta* and, most recently, *The Deepest South of All: True Stories from Natchez, Mississippi*.

JAKI SHELTON GREEN, ninth Poet Laureate of North Carolina, appointed in 2018, is the first African American and third woman to be appointed as the North Carolina Poet Laureate and was reappointed in 2021 for a second term by Governor Roy Cooper. She is a 2019 Academy of American Poet Laureate Fellow, 2014 North Carolina Literary Hall of Fame inductee, 2009 North Carolina Piedmont Laureate appointee, and 2003 recipient of the North Carolina Award for Literature. Green teaches documentary poetry at Duke University Center for Documentary Studies and is the 2021 Frank B. Hanes Writer in Residence at the University of North Carolina at Chapel Hill. Additionally, she received the George School Outstanding Alumni Award in 2021. Her publications include *Dead on Arrival, Masks, Dead on Arrival and New Poems, Conjure Blues, singing a tree into dance*, and *breath of the song*, published by Blair Publishers; *Feeding the Light* and *i want to undie you*, published by Jacar Press; *i want to undie you English /Italian bilingual edition*, published by Lebeg Publishers. Juneteenth 2020, she released her first LP, the poetry album *The River Speaks of Thirst*, produced by Soul City Sounds and Clearly Records, and released a CD, *i want to undie you*, in 2021. Green is the owner of *SistaWRITE* providing writing retreats for women writers in Sedona, Arizona; Martha's Vineyard; Ocracoke, North Carolina; Northern Morocco; and Tullamore, Ireland.

DAVID HOUSTON is the executive director of the Ohr-O'Keefe Museum of Art in Biloxi, Mississippi.

CLEMENTINE HUNTER (1887–1988) painted every day from the 1930s until several days before her death at age 101. She produced between five and ten thousand paintings, ranging from her well-known colorful canvases to glass snuff bottles and discarded roofing shingles, including her most ambitious work, the African House Murals. She spent the first half of her life working in the fields of Louisiana's Melrose Plantation, but it was when she moved to the plantation's Big House and became a cook and domestic servant that her creativity blossomed. Her memory paintings of cotton planting and harvesting, washdays, weddings, births, baptisms, funerals, spirituality, Saturday night revelry, and flowers recall her experiences of everyday plantation life along the Cane River. More than a personal record of Hunter's life, her art also reflects the social, material, and cultural aspects of twentieth-century plantation life in Louisiana's African American community.

CHERYL ISAAC is a Liberian American writer and a survivor of the First Liberian Civil War. She has received fellowships from MacDowell, Tin House, and Disquiet International Writing Workshops. Her work has been published and is forthcoming in *Chicago Quarterly Review, The Common, Ocean State Review, Hawaii Pacific Review, Prime Number, Cosmonauts Avenue*, and other journals.

JOHN JUNG was born in Macon, Georgia, to Chinese immigrant parents who operated a laundry during the years before the civil rights era. He didn't fully know what being Chinese meant as his family were the only Chinese in town. After he retired from a forty-year career as a professor of psychology, his interest in understanding how his ethnic identity emerged led him to write a memoir, *Southern Fried Rice: Life in A Chinese Laundry in the Deep South*, in 2005. Positive responses from readers made him realize this was an important story to preserve and share. He was inspired to write several additional books: *Chinese Laundries: Tickets to Survival on Gold Mountain* (2007), *Chopsticks in the Land of Cotton: Lives of Mississippi Delta Chinese Grocers* (2009), *Sweet & Sour: Life in Chinese Family Restaurants* (2010), *and A Chinese American Odyssey: How a Retired Psychologist Makes a Hit as a Historian* (2014).

MALINDA MAYNOR LOWERY is a historian and documentary film producer who is a member of the Lumbee Tribe. She is the Cahoon Family Professor of American History at Emory University. She is the author of *The Lumbee Indians: An American Struggle* (UNC Press, 2018).

PETER MABLI is a public historian who serves as director of online programs for the American Social History Project at the City University of New York (CUNY) Graduate Center. He is also an adjunct professor of history at Fairleigh Dickinson University where he teaches courses on cultural revolutions and the history of New Jersey. Mabli has a PhD from Drew University, with a focus on the intersections between food culture and national identity creation in the early American Republic.

MICHAEL MALONE is the author of a dozen novels, including *Handling Sin, Dingley Falls*, and *Foolscap*. His book *The Four Corners of the Sky* is the latest of a number of national bestsellers. He has also published a collection of short stories, *Red Clay, Blue Cadillac*, as well as two books of nonfiction (one on American movies, one on Jungian psychology). Television credits include network shows for ABC, NBC, and Fox. His stories, essays, and critical writings have appeared in a wide range of journals and anthologies—among them the *Wilson Quarterly*, the *Partisan Review, Playboy,*

Mademoiselle, Harper's, the *New York Times*, the *Nation* and *The Best American Mystery Stories of the Century*. He's also written plays, musicals and scripts. Among the prizes he has received are the O. Henry, the Edgar, the Writers Guild Award, and the Emmy for ABC's *One Life to Live*, where he was head writer for much of a decade. He has taught at Yale University, the University of Pennsylvania, and Swarthmore College, and has now retired as professor of theater studies and English at Duke University. Currently he is at work on the final "Hillston" novel of a quartet that includes *Uncivil Seasons, Time's Witness*, and *First Lady*. His home is in Hillsborough, North Carolina.

ELIZABETH MATHESON, a native of Hillsborough, North Carolina, earned her BA from Sweet Briar College and later studied at the Penland School of Crafts with John Menapace. One-person exhibitions of her work have been held at Hollins University, the Virginia Polytechnic Institute, the North Carolina Museum of Art, Duke University, Western Carolina University, the National Humanities Center, and the Gregg Museum at North Carolina State University. Her work is in the collections of Duke University, the Ackland Museum, and the North Carolina Museum of Art, among many others. Among her publications are *To See*, poems by Michael McFee; *Blithe Air: Photographs of England, Wales, and Ireland*; and *Shell Castle, Portrait of a North Carolina House*. In 2004, Matheson was awarded the North Carolina Award for Excellence in the Arts, the state's highest civilian honor.

JILL McCORKLE is the author of seven novels (most recent: *Hieroglyphics*) and four story collections. Her work has appeared in numerous periodicals, and four of her short stories have been selected for *The Best American Short Stories*. She has taught at Harvard University, Brandeis University, and North Carolina State University and currently teaches in the Bennington College Writing Seminars. She lives in Hillsborough, North Carolina, with her husband, photographer Tom Rankin.

MARÍA TERESA UNGER PALMER (*Maritere*) came to the United States as an exchange student in 1978, fell in love, married Mike Palmer, and made the South her home. A US citizen since 1987, María has worked for justice as an activist, a bivocational pastor, a public school teacher, a principal, a university administrator, and in elected and appointed positions. María is proud to have an EdD from the University of North Carolina at Chapel Hill, to have founded *Mi Escuelita*, the first Spanish immersion preschool in North Carolina, and to have helped bring language immersion to the public schools of Chapel Hill. Micheal and María live in Chapel Hill, North Carolina, they delight in their first grandchild, Tomás; their three grown children, Cristobal, Benji, and Sofia; and their extended family all over the world.

JAMES L. PEACOCK, retired Kenan Professor of Anthropology at the University of North Carolina at Chapel Hill, was president of the American Anthropological Association from 1993 to 1995. In 1995 he was inducted into the American Academy of

Arts and Sciences, and in 2002 the American Anthropological Association awarded him the prestigious Franz Boas award for Exemplary Service to Anthropology. He conducted fieldwork in Indonesia on the eve of "the year of living dangerously" and with Muhammadiyah, a Muslim organization with thirty million members. His most recent book was *Grounded Globalism: How the U.S. South Embraces the World*, and his ongoing organizational work seeds that embrace. Find out more in his book *A True Lucky Jim*, available on Amazon.

RAMESH RAO flew into Hattiesburg, Mississippi, on September 5, 1985, to begin work on his master's degree in mass communication. With that degree under his belt, he moved to Michigan State University to earn a PhD in communication. Over the past three decades he has taught in Missouri and Virginia and is now professor in the Department of Communication at Columbus State University in Columbus, Georgia. Along the way he has written books on Indian politics and society and a book on intercultural communication for the Indian college student. His articles, essays, and commentaries have appeared in newspapers and magazines such as the *Washington Post*, the *Guardian*, the *St. Louis Post-Dispatch*, *India Abroad*, *India Currents*, *The Pioneer*, *Patheos*, and *Swarajya*. Before boarding that flight to Hattiesburg (via Atlanta, Frankfurt, Mumbai, and Bengaluru), Rao worked as a bank officer, a school teacher, and a copy editor in India. He is still looking for home despite the long roads he has traveled. Rao lives with wife, Sujaya, in Fortson, Georgia, while their son, Sudhanva, pursues a degree in biology and economics at the University of Georgia.

EDWARD RICE was born in 1953 in Augusta, Georgia, and raised in North Augusta, South Carolina. He was protégé of Freeman Schoolcraft from 1972–1979 and Director/Artist in Residence at the Gertrude Herbert Institute of Art, Augusta from 1979–1982. Rice was awarded a South Carolina Arts Commission Artist Fellowship and a National Endowment for the Arts/Southern Arts Federation Regional Fellowship. His work is included in the collections of the Gibbes Museum of Art, the Columbia Museum of Art, the South Carolina State Museum, the Greenville County Museum of Art, the Georgia Museum of Art, the Morris Museum of Art, and the Ogden Museum of Southern Art.

CLAY RISEN is a reporter and editor at the *New York Times* and the author, most recently, of *The Crowded Hour: Theodore Roosevelt, the Rough Riders, and the Dawn of the American Century*. From 2010 to 2020 he was an editor with the *Times*'s opinion section, where among other things he edited Disunion, the paper's online series about the Civil War. He is also the author of several books about whiskey, including the bestseller *American Whiskey, Bourbon and Rye: A Guide to the Nation's Favorite Spirit*, and two other books on American history, *The Bill of the Century: The Epic Battle for the Civil Rights Act* and *A Nation on Fire: America in the Wake of the King Assassination*. He lives in New York City.

WELMON SHARLHORNE was born in New Orleans, Louisiana, in 1952. He spent his childhood in the fields and bayous of Houma, Louisiana, one hour south of New Orleans. After twenty-two years of incarceration for nonviolent crimes, Welmon became recognized as one of the South's leading self-taught artists. Since being released from Angola prison, he lives between New Orleans and Houma, making his distinctive pen and ink drawings that continue to be sought by collectors and museums here and abroad.

KENDALL SHAW (1924–2019) was a New Orleans-born painter whose career has spanned a number of art styles—ranging from abstract expressionism to pop art to minimalism to pattern and design to color field—with heightened emotion, pattern, shape, and vivid color predominant. Shaw's work includes a series of thirty paintings based on the Torah of the Old Testament as well as work with pure colors that he terms "Cajun Minimalism."

VOLLIS SIMPSON (1919–2013) spent most of his ninety-four years living in the house where he was born and died, outside of the community of Lucama, Wilson County, North Carolina, with the exception of a stint in the US Army Air Corps after high school and during World War II. Following the war, Simpson returned to Wilson County where he married and started a family, farmed for a few years, and then opened a repair shop in 1951. In the late 1970s Vollis began constructing large artistic and kinetic windmills and whirligigs, erecting them on land around his repair shop and a nearby pond. Soon he was making commissioned pieces for the American Visionary Art Museum (AVAM) in Baltimore, the Folk Art Park at the 1994 Atlanta Olympics, and the North Carolina Museum of Art in Raleigh, while also selling smaller works to people who came by his repair shop. For more than thirty years, Simpson repurposed scrapped materials into sculptures, transforming a rural five-points intersection into an art environment that people often called Acid Park or The Lights. Simpson challenged simple categorization as craftsman, mechanic, engineer, artist; he combined skill with creative ability to turn the discarded into enormous playful kinetic sculptures.

BILL SMITH is the author of two cookbooks and many articles and essays in various magazines and journals. In 2019 he retired after twenty-five years as head chef at Crook's Corner Restaurant in Chapel Hill, North Carolina. He has received nominations several times from the James Beard Foundation for Best Chef Southeast and served for six years on the board of the Southern Foodways Alliance.

KATY SIMPSON SMITH was born and raised in Jackson, Mississippi. She received a PhD in history from the University of North Carolina at Chapel Hill and an MFA from the Bennington Writing Seminars. She is the author of *We Have Raised All* *of You: Motherhood in the South, 1750–1835,* and the novels *The Story of Land and Sea, Free Men,* and *The Everlasting.* Her writing has also appeared in the *New York Times Book Review, Paris Review, Los Angeles Review of Books, Oxford American, Granta,* and *Literary Hub.* She lives in New Orleans, Louisiana.

LEO TWIGGS was born in St. Stephen, South Carolina. He received his BA from Claflin University, later studied at the Art Institute of Chicago, and received his MA from New York University where he studied with Hale Woodruff, the acclaimed African American painter and muralist. In 1970, Twiggs became the first Black student to receive a Doctorate of Arts from the University of Georgia. He taught at South Carolina State University where he chaired the art department until 1998. Twiggs's work is widely exhibited nationally and internationally in more than seventy-five one-person shows. He was the first visual artist to receive the Verner Award (Governor's Trophy) for outstanding contributions to the arts in South Carolina. In 2018, he received the $10,000 *1858 Prize for Southern Contemporary Painting* and in 2019, the *Larry and Brenda Thompson African American Art Award* at the Georgia Museum of Art. He was inducted into the South Carolina Hall of Fame in 2020. His book, *Messages from Home: The Art of Leo Twiggs,* was published by Claflin University Press in 2011. Find out more at www.leotwiggs.com.

LEWIS WATTS is a photographer, archivist/curator, and professor emeritus of art at the University of California, Santa Cruz. His research and artwork centers primarily around the cultural landscape, focusing on communities of the African diaspora in the San Francisco Bay Area, the South, the Caribbean, Europe, and Africa. His research examines the imprint of migration. He is the coauthor of *Harlem of the West: The San Francisco Fillmore Jazz Era* and *New Orleans Suite: Music and Culture in Transition.* He is also working on extended photographic projects in Charleston, Savannah, and Harlem, New York. His personal website is https://art.ucsc.edu/faculty/lewis-watts.

KATERINA KATSARKA WHITLEY is the author of eight books. Her most recent book is a memoir, *Myth and Memory: My Childhood in WWII Greece.* She studied at Anatolia College in Thessaloniki, Greece, and at Mars Hill College in North Carolina, Furman University, Southeastern Theological Seminary, and East Carolina University. She taught children of all ages, worked as a church journalist in the Diocese of East Carolina for a decade, and at the Episcopal Church Center in New York City for another decade. From her base in New York, she traveled widely in the developing world to collect and tell stories of women and children. After leaving New York she taught communication courses at Appalachian State University for nearly two decades. Her books are *Speaking for Ourselves; Seeing for Ourselves; Walking the Way of Sorrows; Waiting for the Wonder; Light to the Darkness; and A New Love.* Her cookbook on Greek culture and food is *Around a Greek Table: Recipes and Stories.* She has been published in the *Christian Science Monitor*, the Raleigh *News and Observer*, and other publications. Katerina, now widowed, has an extensive schedule as a speaker/performer but cherishes being a mother and grandmother. She lives and writes in Boone, North Carolina.

LYNN YORK is the author of two novels: *The Piano Teacher* (Plume, 2004) and *The Sweet Life* (Plume, 2007), a Booksense Notable Book. A graduate of Duke University and the University of Texas at Austin, she is the publisher at Blair, a Durham-based nonprofit press whose mission is to seek out, nurture, and promote literary works by new and historically excluded writers. Lynn lives in Chapel Hill, North Carolina.